Seminal Sociological Writings, Volume 2:
From Harriet Martineau to W.E.B. Du Bois

Other Notable Gordian Knot Books

Studies in Structural Sociology (2015) by Frank W. Young, PhD

On Being a Woman Surgeon: Sixty Women Share Their Stories (2015) Edited by Preeti R. John, MD

Dancing on the Tails of the Bell Curve: Readings on the Joy and Power of Statistics (2013) Edited by Richard Altschuler, PhD

Doctor, Why Does My Face Still Ache? Getting Relief from Persistent Jaw, Ear, Tooth, and Headache Pain (2012) by Donald R. Tanenbaum, DDS and S. L. Roistacher, DDS

Putting Universal Human Rights to Work: Policy Actions in the Struggle for Social Justice (2012) by Archibald Stuart, PhD

Where Are We Going? (2012) by Miriam Finder Tasini, MD

Reflections on Medicine: Essays by Robert U. Massey, MD (2011) Edited by Martin Duke, MD

Contemplative Aging: A Way of Being in Later Life (2010) by Edmund Sherman, PhD

Seminal Sociological Writings: From Auguste Comte to Max Weber: An Anthology of Groundbreaking Works that Created the Science of Sociology (2010) Edited by Richard Altschuler, PhD

Identifying and Recovering from Psychological Trauma: A Psychiatrist's Guide for Victims of Childhood Abuse, Spousal Battery, and Political Terrorism (2009) by Brian Trappler, MD

Malthus, Darwin, Durkheim, Marx, Weber, Ibn Khaldûn: On Human Species Survival (2009) by Walter L. Wallace, PhD

It's Good to Know a Miracle: Dani's Story: One Family's Struggle with Leukemia (2008) by Jay Shotel, PhD, and Sue Shotel

Hope Springs Maternal: Homeless Mothers Talk about Making Sense of Adversity (2007) by Jill Gerson, DSW

On the Cutting Edge: Tales of a Cold War Engineer at the Dawn of the Nuclear, Guided Missile, Computer, and Space Ages (2006) by Robert Brodsky, PhD

The Living Legacy of Marx, Durkheim & Weber: Applications and Analyses of Classical Sociological Theory by Modern Social Scientists, volumes 1 & 2 (2001) Edited by Richard Altschuler, PhD

Seminal Sociological Writings, Volume 2: From Harriet Martineau to W.E.B. Du Bois

Edited by

Richard Altschuler

Gordian Knot Books

An Imprint of Richard Altschuler & Associates, Inc.

Los Angeles

Seminal Sociological Writings, Volume 2: From Harriet Martineau to W.E.B. Du Bois. Copyright©2014 by Gordian Knot Books. For information contact the publisher at 10390 Wilshire Boulevard, Los Angeles, CA 90024, 424-279-9118, or richard.altschuler@gmail.com.

Library of Congress Control Number: 2014953555
CIP data for this book are available from the Library of Congress

ISBN-13: 978-1-884092-94-7

Cover Design and Layout: Josh Garfield

Printed in the United States of America

To Jane

CONTENTS

Editor's Preface

Between 1830 and 1842 Auguste Comte, a French philosopher, published the *Course on Positive Philosophy* (*Cours de Philosophie Positive*), a six-volume work that gave birth to a new academic discipline: sociology. Although people had been writing about human behaviors and social relationships for thousands of years, it took Comte's revolutionary work to define a "science of society," which he originally referred to as "social physics" before coining the term "sociology" (*sociologie*).

In *Positive Philosophy* Comte took a unique viewpoint of individuals in relationship to one another, understanding that a "social relationship" is different from individual behavior and a "society" is different from a mere collection of individuals. He also took a certain approach or method to study societal phenomena, which he discussed as "positivism." Important as his work was, it may have had little impact in Great Britain and America during the nineteenth century if it were not for Harriet Martineau—the first author featured in this anthology—who translated Comte's work into English in 1853, and published it as a condensed version titled *The Positive Philosophy of Auguste Comte.*

When Comte published his groundbreaking work, only about fifty years had passed since the revolutions in America and France, and these nations and others were undergoing rapid industrialization and giving rise to great cities filled with masses of poor people. In this post-revolutionary environment of rapid social change and disorganization the early founders of sociology emerged.

They were not formally trained or academically credentialed "sociologists," of course, because the discipline of sociology was just developing. Rather, they were intellectuals and social activitists trained in areas such as philosophy, law, religion, politics, and medicine, who had at least one thing in common: They passionately wanted to understand the nature of human societies, individual behavior, and social relationships from an objective viewpoint. To achieve this end, many of them wanted to use the same methodologies that physical scientists used rather than rely on philosophical speculation or religious belief and faith. Other founders of sociology were motivated by a desire to decrease or eradicate poverty or health problems; some sought to apply evolutionary principles drawn from biology in order to justify or explain inequalities in human social life; and still others simply wanted to understand what makes us "tick," among other powerful motivations for creating and developing a "science of society."

Given the newness of sociology, many early pioneers were extremely concerned with defining their new field and its basic concepts, methods, ideas, and theories. They asked fundamental questions such as "How is society possible?" and "What is a social fact?" For about seventy years, the new discipline of sociology grew and blossomed; and by around 1900 the "science of society" had became firmly rooted in college and university departments throughout America, Great Britain, France, Germany, and many other countries.

The Value of Primary Source Documents
If you are interested in the origins of sociology, then reading books *about* the founders and their seminal works can prove to be a rewarding experience. Such "second order" information, however, is no substitute for the experience you will have and the depth of understanding you will gain by reading the original works of the sociological founders, which are presented in this anthology.

These primary source documents will allow you to experience how the groundbreaking thinkers *introduced* the paradigm-changing constructs that both shattered earlier perceptions of reality and dominate how contemporary social scientists think about and study human relationships, institutions, societies, and cultures. In addition to allowing you to "tune in" to the founders' thoughts and reasoning processes *directly,* these primary source documents will give you an invaluable research resource, because they were written by the founders in the first person, as they were undergoing their groundbreaking theoretical insights and discoveries, and while they were recording, reflecting on, witnessing, and living through the phenomena that engaged them as they occurred.

The Founders Included in the Anthology
As you consider the founders of sociology included in this book, you may wonder, "Are they the most important founders?" The answer to this question is that there are many other important founders of sociology than are presented in this volume. If you read the predecessor to this vol-

ume, *Seminal Sociology Writings: From Auguste Comte to Max Weber* (2010), then you know some of the most important founders of sociology are men such as Auguste Comte, Herbert Spencer, Karl Marx, Émile Durkheim, Georg Simmel, and Max Weber, among ten others included in that volume. All of them made invaluable contributions to the theory and methods of sociology. Those sixteen founders were all white men, born in Great Britain, Continental Europe, and America.

This volume adds sixteen more important founders of sociology—including four women and an African-American man—who have made significant, early contributions that helped define and establish the "science of society." As the subtitle of this book says, the writings in this volume span the time from Harriet Martineau—generally acknowledged to be the first woman sociologist—to W.E.B. Du Bois—generally considered to be the first black sociologist. Martineau was born in 1802, before anyone else in this anthology, just a few decades after the signing of the U.S. Constitution and the French Revolution; and Du Bois died later than anyone else in this anthology, in 1963, at the age of 95, on the eve of the Civil Rights March in Washington, DC. While both of them wrote many great, lasting works of importance, the selections chosen for this anthology come from what are, perhaps, considered their greatest works: For Martineau, it is *How to Observe Morals and Manners*, written in 1838, when she was thirty-six years old; and for Du Bois, it is *The Souls of Black Folk*, written in 1903, when he was thirty-five years old. Their lives "bookend" this rich collection of fourteen other sociological pioneers, all of whom were born—like the founders in the first volume—in Great Britain, Continental Europe, or America.

When considering who to include in this second volume, I especially had in mind, as in the first volume, certain seminal works that focus on specific concepts, ideas, and theories that every sociologist, I am certain, would agree help to define the discipline of sociology and its primary concerns. Examples of seminal writings in this category are by William F. Ogburn ("culture lag"), Vilfredo Pareto ("circulation of elites"), and Robert Michels (the "iron law of oligarchy"), among others. I also had in mind, however, to include certain works that both contributed to sociological analysis and were manifestly critical of society in certain major respects, e.g., the unequal power relationships between men and women and between whites and blacks. These authors sought to change social institutions for the betterment of specific societal groups, such as industrial workers, blacks, women, and immigrants. Examples of seminal writings in this category are by Jane Addams, Charlotte Perkins Gilman, and Frederick Engels, in addition to those by Martineau, Du Bois and others.

Collectively, the selections in this anthology, like those of its predecessor, focus on specific questions of primary importance to the discipline of sociology, including the following:

- Can societies achieve democracy or will there always be impediments to its realization that are inherent in the structure and function of societal institutions?
- Is sociology a science like the physical sciences or is it fundamentally different because of its subject matter?
- What is the subject matter of sociology and how is it different from that of other disciplines concerned with human behavior, such as history, anthropology, and political science?
- What are social classes and must they inherently be in a state of conflict?
- Does the institution of the family discriminate against women and account for their unequal position relative to men in society?
- What effect does the economic system of a society have on the relationship between the sexes?
- What factors account for the rise of the modern nation-state?
- What are the functions of customs, folkways and mores and how do they affect social life in all societies?
- What are social facts and how are they different from physical facts and psychological facts?
- What is applied sociology and how can it be used to help solve our most severe societal problems?

The founders of sociology asked and answered these and related questions with dazzling displays of imagination, intellectual prowess, vision, and, in some instances, "hard data" and methodological rigor.

Presentation of the Chapters, Citations, and Additional References
The body of the book is divided into sixteen chapters, one for each founder of sociology, beginning with Harriet Martineau (1802-1876) and

ending with W.E.B. Du Bois (1868-1963). At the beginning of each chapter, the reader is provided with the "source" of the seminal writing to be presented (e.g., a book and its original year of publication) and the "selection" from the source (e.g., a chapter from the book), followed by an "Introduction" about the background of the author and significance of the writing for the discipline of sociology.

After the last chapter, the "References" section provides complete bibliographic information for each work in the anthology, followed by the "Additional Recommended Books, Articles and Websites" section, for readers interested in learning more about the founders of sociology and their work.

Notes on Editing

I have taken great care to present the writings as they appear in the source documents, to the maximum extent possible. It was necessary at times, however, to make certain minor edits to the text, in order to give contemporary readers a comprehensible, relevant experience, and also to give this book a uniformity of style. Thus, in some instances I made the following changes with regard to punctuation, spelling, word usage, deletions, emphasized words, and footnotes:

Punctuation: I have retained the punctuation in the original source works except in rare instances when they contain errors, such as run-on sentences or sentence fragments, which make comprehension difficult.

Spelling: I have corrected spelling errors contained in the source works but retained almost all British and archaic spellings of English words, such as "honour," "connexions," and "civilisation," among others, as long as I felt they would be comprehensible to a modern reader.

Inconsistencies of style or word usage: In rare instances the authors used spellings or capitalization inconsistently. I have retained such inconsistencies in this volume, except in those instances when I felt they interfered with comprehension or readability.

Emphasized text: In some of the selections, the authors chose to call attention to words or phrases by using capitalization, italics, or other text attributes. I have retained such attributes and have not emphasized any text not emphasized in the source documents.

Deletions: In a few of the selections I have deleted some body text or footnotes, for one of three reasons: (a) the text is an "aside" to the content of the writing that does not add anything to the main argument; (b) the text presents examples so historically specific about people, places, or events in the 1800s or early 1900s that modern readers would be unlikely to relate to them or find them relevant; (c) the text is redundant without adding anything of substantive value to the main argument. In no instance was text in the body of a selection deleted that I felt would detract from the major contribution of the writer or the selection chosen for this anthology. When such text has been deleted, it is indicated by an ellipsis (. . .).

Uniformity of Appearance and Style: Each of the sixteen source documents in this anthology was originally published with different formatting and typestyles, of course, and the same is true of their subsequent reprintings in books and journals. To eliminate such variation and give this book a uniformity of appearance and style, I have presented all the selections with the same formatting and typeface attributes.

A Few Final Thoughts

Some of the selections in this anthology have a more "formal" feel than we are used to in much contemporary writing, e.g., in terms of their syntax and vocabulary, largely because they were written between the early nineteenth century and early twentieth century. When you come across such a selection, I suggest you read it more slowly, i.e., with a bit more patience, than you might read a less formal, more modern sounding text, to give yourself a chance to get acclimated to the style of writing.

No matter how you experience the style or "feel" of a given text, however, you may be surprised to see how pertinent every selection is for understanding modern societies and our own lives within them. In other words, these seminal works about "culture lag" "class conflict," "elites," "collective bargaining," and other topics written decades ago may be "old" but they are not "dated."

With the above in mind, happy reading!

Harriet Martineau
1802–1876

Source: *How to Observe Morals and Manners* (1838)
Selection: "Marriage and Woman"

Introduction: *Harriet Martineau is often called the "founding mother" of sociology for both her theoretical and empirical work. She was born in Norwich, England, the sixth of eight children, to a family of French Heugenot ancestry. Her father was a manufacturer and her mother was the daughter of a sugar refiner. At a young age, Martineau began to lose her sense of taste and smell, and soon thereafter had to use an ear trumpet because she became increasingly deaf.*

Her writing career began at about the age of twenty, and throughout her life she was a prolific writer. Her publications include twenty-five didactic novels, in a series called Illustrations of Political Economy; *the first sociological research text,* How to Observe Morals and Manners; *three volumes on her field work in the United States titled* Society in America; *and a book on her research in the Middle East called* Eastern Life: Present and Past. *She also translated and edited Auguste Comte's* Positive Philosophy *from French to English—a book many claim is the first to define the discipline of sociology. Her translation was so highly acclaimed that Comte translated her rendition of his book back into French.*

To Martineau, the central concern of sociology was what she called "social life in society"—the patterns, causes, consequences, and problems of the social world. In keeping with Comte and other sociological founders at the time, such as Herbert Spencer, she was a "positivist" who believed in social laws and the progressive evolution of society. Even before the works of Marx, Durkheim, or Weber, Martineau examined sociological phenomena such as social class, religion, suicide, and domestic relations, and analyzed their impact on individuals' social problems. She also fought for women's and workers' rights and an end to slavery and religious intolerance. According to Martineau, the most important law of social life is human happiness, and in much of her work she sought to understand the extent to which individuals developed "morals and manners" to achieve this end.

Martineau used a comparative methodological approach to study the moral principles in different societies and to uncover the degrees to which these societies had progressed. She devised three measures to study pro-

gress, including the condition of the less powerful groups in society, the cultural attitudes towards authority and autonomy, and the extent to which all individuals were provided the tools to realize autonomous moral action. Unlike Herbert Spencer, Martineau was overwhelmingly concerned with the phenomenon of inequality, especially as it was reflected in gender, race, and class. When researching the moral condition of America, for example, she focused on marriage patterns and criticized the subservient role of women, as may be seen in the following reading from one of her best known and influential books, How to Observe Morals and Manners.

*

The marriage compact is the most important feature of the domestic state on which the observer can fix his attention. If he be a thinker, he will not be surprised at finding much imperfection in the marriage state wherever he goes. By no arrangements yet attempted have purity of morals, constancy of affection, and domestic peace been secured to any extensive degree in society. Almost every variety of method is still in use, in one part of the world or another. . . . Law and opinion have, however, never availed to anything like complete success. Even in thriving young countries, where no considerations of want, and few of ambition, can interfere with domestic peace—where the numbers are equal, where love has the promise of a free and even course, and where religious sentiment is directed full upon the sanctity of the marriage state—it is found to be far from pure. In almost all countries, the corruption of society in this department is so deep and wide-spreading, as to vitiate both moral sentiment and practice in an almost hopeless degree. It neutralizes almost all attempts to ameliorate and elevate the condition of the race. There must be something fearfully wrong where the general result is so unfortunate as this. As in most other cases of social suffering, the wrong will be found to lie less in the methods ordained and put in practice, than in the prevalent sentiment of society, out of which all methods arise.

It is necessary to make mention (however briefly) of the kinds of false sentiment from which the evil of conjugal unhappiness appears to spring. The sentiment by which courage is made the chief ground of honour in men, and chastity in women, coupled with the inferiority in which women have ever been sunk, was sure to induce profligacy. As long as men were brave nothing more was required to make them honourable in the eyes of society: while the inferior condition of women has ever exposed those of them who were not protected by birth and wealth to the profligacy of men. The shallowness of the sentiment of honour is another great evil. In its origin, honour includes self-respect and the respect of others. . . . The requisitions of honour come to be viewed as regarding only equals, or those who are hedged about with honour, and they are neglected with regard to the helpless. Men of honour use treachery with women—with those to whom they promise marriage, and with those to whom, in marrying, they promised fidelity, love, and care; and yet their honour is, in the eyes of society, unstained. Feudal ambition is another sentiment fraught with evil to marriage. In a society where pride and ostentation prevail, where rank and wealth are regarded as prime objects of pursuit, marriage comes to be regarded as a means of obtaining these. Wives are selected for their connexions and their fortune, and the love is placed elsewhere. Any one of these corrupt species of sentiment, and of some others which exist, must ruin domestic peace, if the laws of each country were as wise as they are now, for the most part, faulty, and as powerful as they are now ineffectual. If the traveller will bear these things in mind, he will gain light upon the moral sentiment of the society by the condition of domestic life in it; and again, what he knows of the prevalent moral sentiment of the society will cast light upon the domestic condition of its members.

Marriage exists everywhere, to be studied by the moral observer. He must watch the character of courtships wherever he goes. . . . He must observe how fate is defied by lovers in various countries. . . . He must note the degree of worldly ambition which attends marriages, and which may therefore be supposed to stimulate them—how much space the house with two rooms in humble life, and the country-seat and carriages in higher life, occupy in the mind of bride or bridegroom. He must observe whether conjugal infidelity excites horror and rage, or whether it is so much a matter of course as that no jealousy interferes to mar the arrangements of mutual convenience. He must mark whether women are made absolutely the property of their husbands, in mind and in estate; or whether the wife is treated more or less professedly as an equal party in the agreement. He must observe whether there is an excluded class, victims to their own superstition or to a false social obligation, wandering about to disturb by their jealousy or licentiousness those whose lot is happier. He must observe whether there are domestic arrangements for home enjoyments, or whether all is planned on the supposition of pleasure lying abroad; whether the reliance is on books, gardens, and play with children, or on the opera, parties, the ale-house, or dances on the green. He must mark whether the ladies are occupied with their household cares in the morning, and the society of their husbands in the evening, or with embroidery and looking out of balconies; with receiving company all day, or gadding abroad; with the library or the nursery; with lovers or with children. In each country, called civilized, he will meet with almost all these varieties: but in each there is such a prevailing character in the aspect of domestic life, that intelligent observation will enable him to decide, without much danger of mistake, as to whether marriage is merely an arrangement of convenience, in accordance with low morals, or a sacred institution, commanding the reverence and affection of a virtuous people. No high degree of this sanctity can be looked for till that moderation is attained which, during the prevalence of asceticism and its opposite, is reached only by a few. That it yet exists nowhere as the characteristic of any society—that all the blessings of domestic life are not yet open to all, so as to preclude the danger of any one encroaching on his neighbour—is but too evident to the travelled observer. He can only mark the degree of approximation to this state of high morals wherever he goes.

The traveller everywhere finds woman treated as the inferior party in a compact in which both parties have an equal interest. Any agreement thus formed is imperfect, and is liable to disturbance; and the danger is great in proportion to the degradation of the supposed weaker party. The degree of the degradation of woman is as good a test as the moralist can adopt for ascertaining the state of domestic morals in any country.

The Indian squaw carries the household burdens, trudging in the dust, while her husband on horseback paces before her, unencumbered but by his own gay trappings. She carries the wallet with food, the matting for the lodge, the merchandize (if they possess any), and her infant. There is no exemption from labour for the squaw of the most vaunted chief. In other countries the wife may be found drawing the plough, hewing wood and carrying water; the men of the family standing idle to witness her toils. Here the observer may feel pretty sure of his case. From a condition of slavery like this, women are found rising to the highest condition in which they are at present seen, in France, England, and the United States—where they are less than half-educated, precluded from earning a subsistence, except in a very few ill-paid employments, and prohibited from giving or withholding their assent to laws which they are yet bound by penalties to obey. In France, owing to the great destruction of men in the wars of Napoleon, women are engaged, and successfully engaged, in a variety of occupations which have been elsewhere supposed unsuitable to the sex. Yet there remains so large a number who cannot, by the most strenuous labour in feminine employments, command the necessaries of life, while its luxuries may be earned by infamy, that the morals of the society are naturally bad. Great attention has of late been given to this subject in France: the social condition of women is matter of thought and discussion to a degree which promises some considerable amelioration. Already, women can do more in France than anywhere else; they can attempt more without ridicule or arbitrary hinderance: and the women of France are probably destined to lead the way in the advance which the sex must hereafter make. At present, society is undergoing a transition from a feudal state to one of mutual government; and women, gaining in some ways, suffer in others during the process. They have, happily for themselves, lost much of the peculiar kind of observance which was the most remarkable feature of the chivalrous age; and it has been impossible to prevent their sharing in the benefits of the improvement and diffusion of knowledge. All cultivation of their powers has secured to them the use of new power; so that their condition is far superior to what it was in any former age. But new difficulties about securing a maintenance have arisen. Marriage is less general; and the husbands of the greater number of women are not secure of a maintenance from the lords of the soil, any more than women are from being married. The charge of their own maintenance is thrown upon large numbers of women, without the requisite variety of employments having been opened to them, or the needful education imparted. A natural consequence of this is that women are educated to consider marriage the one object in life, and therefore to be extremely impatient to secure it. The unfavourable influence of these results upon the happiness of domestic life may be seen at a glance.

This may be considered the sum and substance of female education in England; and the case is scarcely better in France, though the independence and practical efficiency of women there are greater than in any other country. The women in the United States are in a lower condition than either, though there is less striving after marriage, from its greater frequency, and little restriction is imposed upon the book-learning which women may obtain. But the old feudal notions about the sex flourish there, while they are going out in the more advanced countries of Europe; and these notions, in reality, regulate the condition of women. American women generally are treated in no degree as equals, but with a kind of superstitious outward observance, which, as they have done nothing to earn it, is false and hurtful. Coexisting with this, there is an extreme difficulty in a woman's obtaining a maintenance, except by the exercise of some rare powers. In a country where women are brought up to be indulged wives, there is no hope, help, or prospect for such as have not money and are not married.

In America, women can earn a maintenance only by teaching, sewing, employment in factories, keeping boarding-houses, and domestic service. Some governesses are tolerably well paid—comparing their earnings with those of men. Employment in factories, and domestic service, are well paid. Sewing is so wretched an occupation everywhere that it is to be hoped that machinery will soon supersede the use of human fingers in a labour so unprofitable. In Boston, Massachusetts, a woman is paid ninepence (sixpence English) for making a shirt. In England, besides these occupations, others are opening; and, what is of yet greater consequence, the public mind is awakening to the necessity of enlarging the sphere of female industry. Some of the inferior branches of the fine arts have lately offered profitable employment to many women. The commercial adversity to which the country has been exposed from time to time has been of service to the sex, by throwing hundreds and thousands of them upon their own resources, and thus impelling them to urge claims and show powers which are more respected every day. In France this is yet more conspicuously the case. There, women are shop-keepers, merchants, professional accountants, editors of newspapers, and employed in many other ways, unexampled elsewhere, but natural and respectable enough on the spot.

Domestic morals are affected in two principal respects by these differences. Where feminine occupations of a profitable nature are few, and therefore overstocked, and therefore yielding a scanty maintenance with difficulty, there is the strongest temptation to prefer luxury with infamy to hardship with unrecognized honour. Hence arises much of the corruption of cities—less in the United States than in Europe, from the prevalence of marriage—but awful in extent everywhere. Where vice is made to appear the interest of large classes of women, the observer may be quite sure that domestic morals will be found impure. If he can meet with any society where the objects of life are as various and as freely open to women as to men, there he may be sure of finding the greatest amount of domestic purity and peace; for, if women were not helpless, men would find it far less easy to be vicious.

The other way in which domestic morals are affected by the scope which is allowed to the powers of women is through the views of marriage which are induced. Marriage is debased by being considered the one worldly object in life—that on which maintenance, consequence, and power depend. Where the husband marries for connexion, fortune, or an heir to his estate, and the wife for an establishment, for consequence, or influence, there is no foundation for high domestic morals and lasting peace; and in a country where marriage is made the single aim of all women, there is no security against the influence of some of these motives even in the simplest and purest cases of attachment. The sordidness is infused from the earliest years; the taint is in the mind before the attachment begins, before the objects meet; and the evil effects upon the marriage state are incalculable.

All this—the sentiment of society with regard to Woman and to Marriage, the social condition of Woman, and the consequent tendency and aim of her education—the traveller must carefully observe. Each civilized society claims for itself the superiority in its treatment of woman. In one, she is indulged with religious shows, and with masquerades, or Punch, as an occasional variety. In another, she is left in honourable and undisputed possession of the housekeeping department. In a third, she is allowed to meddle, behind the scenes, with the business which is confided to her husband's management. In a fourth, she is satisfied in being the cherished domestic companion, unaware of the injury of being doomed to the narrowness of mind which is the portion of those who are always confined to the domestic circle. In a fifth, she is flattered at being guarded and indulged as a being requiring incessant fostering, and too feeble to take care of herself. In a sixth society, there may be found expanding means of independent occupation, of responsible employment for women; and here, other circumstances being equal, is the best promise of domestic fidelity and enjoyment.

It is a matter of course that women who are furnished with but one object—marriage—must be as unfit for anything when their aim is accomplished as if they had never had any object at all. They are no more equal to the task of education than to that of governing the state; and, if any unexpected turn of adversity befalls them, they have no resource but a convent or some other charitable provision. Where, on the other hand, women are brought up capable of maintaining an independent existence, other objects remain when the grand one is accomplished. Their independence of mind places them beyond the reach of the spoiler; and their cultivated faculty of reason renders them worthy guardians of the rational beings whose weal or woe is lodged in their hands. There is yet, as may be seen by a mere glance over society, only a very imperfect provision made anywhere for doing justice to the next generation by qualifying their mothers; but the observer of morals may profit by marking the degrees in which this imperfection approaches to barbarism. Where he finds that girls are committed to convents for education, and have no alternative in life but marriage, in which their will has no share, and a return to their convent, he may safely conclude that there a plurality of lovers is a matter of course, and domestic enjoyments of the highest kind undesired and unknown. He may conclude that as are the parents, so will be the children; and that, for one more generation at least, there will be little or no improvement. But where he finds a variety of occupations open to women; where he perceives them not only pursuing the lighter mechanic arts, dispensing charity and organizing schools for the poor, but occupied in education, and in the study of science and the practice of the fine arts, he may conclude that here resides the highest domestic enjoyment which has yet been attained, and the strongest hope of a further advance.

Frederick Engels
1820-1895

Source: *The Origin of the Family, Private Property and the State* (1884)
Selection: "Barbarism and Civilization"

Introduction: *Frederick Engels was a German sociologist, political theorist, and philosopher most well known for his monumental works with Karl Marx, including* The Communist Manifesto *and* Das Kapital *(of which he edited the second and third volumes after Marx's death). Because he helped to integrate parts of that work and expand its utility to fields beyond merely economics, he is generally viewed as a key influence in the growth of Marxism that led to the establishment of dialectical materialism and the foundation of modern communism. Among his most noted works are* The Condition of the Working Class in England *(1844),* Socialism: Utopian and Scientific *(1880), and* The Origin of the Family, Private Property and the State *(1884).*

Engels developed his proclivity for dialectical thinking and communism as a young adult, even though his father was a businessman—the owner of a textile factory and a partner in a cotton plant in Manchester. From reading works by the philosopher Hegel, Engels' radical leanings intensified. As he became acutely aware of the terrible conditions of the working class, he decided that the only logical path was to promote communism. In 1842, while in Manchester, he took notes on child labor, the environment, and the general life of the laborers, which eventually became published as The Condition of the Working Class in England; *and he met an Irish worker named Mary Burns with whom he had a nonmarital relationship—as he did not believe in the institution of marriage—that lasted until she died in 1862.*

In 1844, after Engels had met with Marx several times (near Manchester and in Cologne and Paris), Marx edited two articles by Engels that presented an incipient form Engels' ideas on scientific socialism. In particular, these papers outlined how private property was a major flaw in the liberal economic system. From 1845 to 1848, Engels and Marx attempted to organize German workers in Brussels—following the way English and French workers were organizing—as revolution was breaking out in many European countries. They joined the German Communist League and, at that point, wrote a "manifesto" for the organization that became the renowned Communist Manifesto.

Frederick Engels

Upon his return to England, Engels' funds had run out, and he realized that Marx had much work to accomplish with his major work Das Kapital. *He therefore decided to return to his family's business in Manchester and accept a position similar to one he had in his adolescence, so that he could continue to send Marx money. He also assisted Marx on a few of his articles during that time, and was especially contributory on matters pertaining to business, economics, military matters, and international questions. In 1869, Engels sold his partnership and the next year moved to London where he and Marx were able to work together until Marx's death in 1883.*

From then on, Engels worked to keep the "Marxist faith" alive, corresponding with German Social Democrats and other followers. He also completed the second and third volumes of Das Kapital, *based on Marx's extensive notes; and published more of his own works, most notably* The Origin of the Family, Private Property and the State *(1884), which contains the following reading from the chapter "Barbarism and Civilization."*

*

The state is the result of the desire to keep down class conflicts. But having arisen amid these conflicts, it is as a rule the state of the most powerful economic class that by force of its economic supremacy becomes also the ruling political class and thus acquires new means of subduing and exploiting the oppressed masses. The antique state was, therefore, the state of the slave owners for the purpose of holding the slaves in check. The feudal state was the organ of the nobility for the oppression of the serfs and dependent farmers. The modern representative state is the tool of the capitalist exploiters of wage labor. At certain periods it occurs exceptionally that the struggling classes balance each other so nearly that the public power gains a certain degree of independence by posing as the mediator between them. . . .

In most of the historical states, the rights of the citizens are differentiated according to their wealth. This is a direct confirmation of the fact that the state is organized for the protection of the possessing against the non-possessing classes. The Athenian and Roman classification by incomes shows this. It is also seen in the medieval state of feudalism in which the political power depended on the quantity of real estate. It is again seen in the electoral qualifications of the modern representative state. The political recognition of the differences in wealth is by no means essential. On the contrary, it marks a low stage of state development. The highest form of the state, the democratic republic, knows officially nothing of property distinctions. It is that form of the state which under modern conditions of society becomes more and more an unavoidable necessity. The last decisive struggle between proletariat and bourgeoisie can only be fought out under this state form. In such a state, wealth exerts its power indirectly, but all the more safely. This is done partly in the form of direct corruption of officials, after the classical type of the United States, or in the form of an alliance between government and bankers, which is established all the more easily when the public debt increases and when corporations concentrate in their hands not only the means of transportation but also production itself, using the stock exchange as a center. The United States and the latest French republic are striking examples, and good old Switzerland has contributed its share to illustrate this point. . . . For as long as the oppressed class, in this case the proletariat, is not ripe for its economic emancipation, just so long will its majority regard the existing order of society as the only one possible, and form the tail, the extreme left wing, of the capitalist class. But the more the proletariat matures toward its self-emancipation, the more does it constitute itself as a separate class and elect its own representatives in place of the capitalists. Universal suffrage is the gauge of the maturity of the working class. It can and will never be anything else but that in the modern state. But that is sufficient. On the day when the thermometer of universal suffrage reaches its boiling point among the laborers, they as well as the capitalists will know what to do.

The state, then, did not exist from all eternity. There have been societies without it that had no idea of any state or public power. At a certain stage of economic development, which was of necessity accompanied by a division of society into classes, the state became the inevitable result of this division. We are now rapidly approaching a stage of evolution in production, in which the existence of classes has not only ceased to be a necessity, but becomes a positive fetter on production. Hence these classes must fall as inevitably as they once arose. The state must irrevocably fall with them. The society that is to reorganize production on the basis of a free and equal association of the producers will transfer the machinery of state, where it will then belong: into the Museum of Antiquities by the side of the spinning wheel and the bronze ax.

Civilization is, as we have seen, that stage of society in which the division of labor, the resulting exchange between individuals, and the production of commodities combining them reach their highest development and revolutionize the whole society.

The production of all former stages of society was mainly collective, and consumption was carried on by direct division of products within more or less small communes. This collective production was confined within the narrowest limits. But it implied the control of production and of the products by the producers. They knew what became of their product: it did not leave their hands until it was consumed by them. As long as production moved on this basis, it could not grow beyond the control of the producers, and it could not create any strange ghostly forces against them. Under civilization, however, this is the inevitable rule.

Into the simple process of production the division of labor was gradually interpolated. It undermined the communism of production and consumption, it made the appropriation of products by single individuals the prevailing rule, and thus introduced the exchange between individuals, in the manner mentioned above. Gradually, the production of commodities became the rule.

This mode of production for exchange, not for home consumption, necessarily passes the products on from hand to hand. The producer gives his product away in exchange. He does no longer know what becomes of it. With the advent of money and of the trader who steps in as a middleman between the producers, the process of exchange becomes still more complicated. The fate of the products becomes still more uncertain. The number of merchants is great and one does not know what the other is doing. The products now pass not only from hand to hand, but also from market to market. The producers have lost the control of the aggregate production in their sphere of life, and the merchants have not yet acquired this control. Products and production become the victims of chance. But chance is only one pole of an interrelation, the other pole of which is called necessity. In nature, where chance seems to reign also, we have long ago demonstrated the innate necessity and law that determines the course of chance on every line. But what is true of nature holds also good of society. Whenever a social function or a series of social processes become too powerful for the control of man, whenever they grow beyond the grasp of man and seem to be left to mere chance, then the peculiar and innate laws of such processes shape the course of chance with increased elementary necessity. Such laws also control the vicissitudes of the production and exchange of commodities. For the individual producer and exchanger, these laws are strange and often un-known forces, the nature of which must be laboriously investigated and ascertained. These economic laws of production are modified by the different stages of this form of production. But generally speaking, the entire period of civilization is dominated by these laws. To this day, the product controls the producer. To this day, the aggregate production of society is managed, not on a uniform plan, but by blind laws that rule with elementary force and find their final expression in the storms of periodical commercial crises.

We have seen that human labor power is enabled at a very early stage of production to produce considerably more than is needed to maintain the producer. We have found that this stage coincided in gen-eral with the first appearance of the division of labor and of exchange between individuals. Now, it was not long before the great truth was discovered that man may himself be a commodity, and that human labor power may be exchanged and exploited by transforming a man into a slave. Hardly had exchange between men been established, when men themselves were also exchanged. The active asset became a passive lia-bility, whether man wanted it or not.

Slavery, which reaches its highest development in civilization, introduced the first great division of an exploited and an exploiting class into society. This division continued during the whole period of civilization. Slavery is the first form of exploitation, characteristic of the antique world. Then followed feudalism in the middle ages, and wage labor in recent times. These are the three great forms of servitude, char-acteristic of the three great epochs of civilization. Their invariable mark is either open or, in modern times, disguised slavery.

The stage of commodity production introducing civilization is marked economically by the introduction of (1) metal coins and, thus, of money as capital, of interest, and of usury; (2) merchants as middlemen between producers; (3) private property and mortgage; (4) slave labor as the prevailing form of production. The form of the family corresponding to civilization and becoming its pronounced custom is monogamy, the supremacy of man over woman, and the monogamous family as the economic unit of society. The aggregation of civilized society is the state, which throughout all typical periods is the state of the ruling class, and in all cases mainly a machine for controlling the oppressed and exploited class. Civilization is furthermore characterized on one side by the permanent introduction of the contrast between city and country as the basis of the entire division of social labor; on the other side by the introduction of the testament by which the property holder is enabled to dispose of his property beyond the hour of his death. This institution is a direct blow at the gentile constitution, and was unknown in Athens until the time of Solon. In Rome it was introduced very early, but we do not know when. In Germany it was originated by the priests in order that the honest German might bequeath his property to the church without any interference.

With this fundamental constitution, civilization had accomplished things for which the old gentile society was no match whatever. But these exploits were accomplished by playing on the most sordid passions and instincts of man, and by developing them at the expense of all his other gifts. Barefaced covetousness was the moving spirit of civilization from its first dawn to the present day; wealth, and again wealth, and for the third time wealth; wealth, not of society, but of the puny individual, was its only and final aim. If nevertheless the advanced development of science, and at repeated times the highest flower of art, fell into its lap, this was only due to the fact that without them the highest emoluments of modern wealth would have been missing. Exploitation of one class by another being the basis of civilization, its whole development involves a continual contradiction. Every progress of production is at the same time a retrogression in the condition of the oppressed class, that is, of the great majority. Every benefit for one class is necessarily an evil for the other, every new emancipation of one class a new oppression for the other. The most drastic proof of this is furnished by the introduction of machinery, the effects of which are well known to-day. And while there is hardly any distinction between rights and duties among barbarians, as we have seen, civilization makes the difference between these two plain even to the dullest mind. For now one class has nearly all the rights, the other class nearly all the duties.

But this is not admitted. What is good for the ruling class is alleged to be good for the whole of society with which the ruling class identifies itself. The more civilization advances, the more it is found to cover with the cloak of charity the evils necessarily created by it, to excuse them or to deny their existence, in short to introduce a conventional hypocrisy that culminates in the declaration: The exploitation of the oppressed class is carried on by the exploiting class solely in the interest of the exploited class itself. And if the latter does not recognize this, but even becomes rebellious, it is simply the worst ingratitude to its benefactors, the exploiters.

Henry Sumner Maine
1822-1888

Source: *Ancient Law* (1861)
Selection: "Legal Fictions" and "The Early History of Contract"

Introduction: *Sir Henry James Sumner Maine, the son of a British physician, was a social scientist, jurist, and legal historian who made major contributions to sociological theory. Writing in the intellectual climate of nineteenth-century "social evolutionism," Maine's major contention was that societies have changed from being based on "status" to being based on "contract." He developed his thesis most fully in* Ancient Law *(1861), a work that compared and contrasted early societies with later "progressive," complex societies. Conceiving the two types of societies as ideal-type polar opposites, he claimed that social relations in early societies were dominated by status—exemplified by obeisance to tradition and kinship—whereas social relations in "progressive" societies are determined by contract—exemplified by individual obligations that stem from voluntary agreements between individuals. In* Ancient Law, *Maine also focused on analyzing the process that allowed for modification of the forms of law in the two types of societies—from archaic law in early societies to the growth of modern law in progressive or complex societies.*

By the early twentieth century, many social scientists, particularly anthropologists, were criticizing Maine's theory of comparative law because of the methodology he used: He relied almost exclusively on materials about ancient Greece and Rome—from which he deduced a hypothetical state of universal social organization—but had little or nothing to say about the customs and laws in any known "primitive" or subsequent "progressive" western society.

Despite criticism of his work, and the widespread condemnation of all social evolutionists of the late nineteenth century, Maine's conceptualization of "ideal polar types" continued to influence major social theorists and affect the course of French, German, and American sociology. Émile Durkheim, for example, used it to contrast societies based on "mechanical solidarity" with societies based on "organic solidarity"; and Ferdinand Tönnies used it to contrast the societal opposites of "Gemeinschaft" and "Gesellschaft."

Today, interest in Maine is being renewed for several reasons, including extensive study of village communities in India and Africa and problems associated with the economic and social growth of recently independent, developing nations.

In the excerpts below from Ancient Law, *we can see how Maine used his ideal type polar opposites to analyze differences between law in early societies (based on "code") and modern societies (based on "contract") under three conceptual rubrics: "fictions," "equity," and "legislation."*

*

Legal Fictions: When primitive law has once been embodied in a Code, there is an end to what may be called its spontaneous development. Henceforward the changes effected in it, if effected at all, are effected deliberately and from without. It is impossible to suppose that the customs of any race or tribe remained unaltered during the whole of the long—in some instances the immense—interval between their declaration by a patriarchal monarch and their publication in writing. It would be unsafe too to affirm that no part of the alteration was effected deliberately. But from the little we know of the progress of law during this period, we are justified in assuming that set purpose had the very smallest share in producing change. Such innovations on the earliest usages as disclose themselves appear to have been dictated by feelings and modes of thought which, under our present mental conditions, we are unable to comprehend. A new era begins, however, with the Codes. Wherever, after this epoch, we trace the course of legal modification, we are able to attribute it to the conscious desire of improvement, or at all events of compassing objects other than those which were aimed at in the primitive times.

It may seem at first sight that no general propositions worth trusting can be elicited from the history of legal systems subsequent to the codes. The field is too vast. We cannot be sure that we have included a sufficient number of phenomena in our observations, or that we accurately understand those which we have observed. But the undertaking will be seen to be more feasible if we consider that, after the epoch of codes, the distinction between stationary and progressive societies begins to make itself felt. It is only with the progressive that we are concerned, and nothing is more remarkable than their extreme fewness. In spite of overwhelming evidence, it is most difficult for a citizen of Western Europe to bring thoroughly home to himself the truth that the civilisation which surrounds him is a rare exception in the history of the world. The tone of thought common among us, all our hopes, fears, and speculations, would be materially affected, if we had vividly before us the relation of the progressive races to the totality of human life. It is indisputable that much the greatest part of mankind has never shown a particle of desire that its civil institutions should be improved since the moment when external completeness was first given to them by their embodiment in some permanent record. One set of usages has occasionally been vio-lently overthrown and superseded by another; here and there a primitive code, pretending to a supernatural origin, has been greatly extended, and distorted into the most surprising forms, by the perversity of sacerdotal commentators; but, except in a small section of the world, there has been nothing like the gradual amelioration of a legal system. There has been material civilisation, but, instead of the civilisation expanding the law, the law has limited the civilisation. The study of races in their primitive condition affords us some clue to the point at which the development of certain societies has stopped. . . .

I confine myself in what follows to the progressive societies. With respect to them it may be laid down that social necessities and social opinion are always more or less in advance of Law. We may come in-definitely near to the closing of the gap between them, but it has a per-petual tendency to reopen. Law is stable; the societies we are speaking of are progressive. The greater or less happiness of a people depends on the degree of promptitude with which the gulf is narrowed.

A general proposition of some value may be advanced with respect to the agencies by which Law is brought into harmony with society. These instrumentalities seem to me to be three in number, Legal Fictions, Equity, and Legislation. Their historical order is that in which I have placed them. Sometimes two of them will be seen operating together, and there are legal systems which have escaped the influence of one or other of them. But I know of no instance in which the order of their appearance has been changed or inverted. The early history of one of them, Equity, is universally obscure, and hence it may be thought by some that certain isolated statutes, reformatory of the civil law, are older than any equi-table jurisdiction. My own belief is that remedial Equity is everywhere older than remedial Legislation; but, should this be not strictly true, it would only be necessary to limit the proposition respecting their order of sequence to the periods at which they exercise a sustained and substantial influence in transforming the original law.

I employ the word "fiction" in a sense considerably wider than that in which English lawyers are accustomed to use it, and with a meaning much more extensive than that which belonged to the Roman "*fictiones.*" *Fictio*, in old Roman law, is properly a term of pleading, and signifies a false averment on the part of the plaintiff which the defendant was not allowed to traverse; such, for example, as an averment that the plaintiff was a Roman citizen, when in truth he was a foreigner. The object of these "*fictions*" was, of course, to give jurisdiction. . . . It is not difficult to understand why fictions in all their forms are particularly congenial to the infancy of society. They satisfy the desire for improvement, which is not quite wanting, at the same time that they do not offend the superstitious disrelish for change which is always present. At a particular stage of social progress they are invaluable expedients for overcoming the rigidity of law, and, indeed, without one of them, the Fiction of Adoption which permits the family tie to be artificially created, it is difficult to understand how society would ever have escaped from its swaddling clothes, and taken its first steps towards civilisation. . . .

The next instrumentality by which the adaptation of law to social wants is carried on I call Equity, meaning by that word any body of rules existing by the side of the original civil law, founded on distinct principles and claiming incidentally to supersede the civil law in virtue of a superior sanctity inherent in those principles. The Equity whether of the Roman *Prætors* [magistrates] or of the English Chancellors, differs from the Fictions which in each case preceded it, in that the interference with law is open and avowed. On the other hand, it differs from Legislation, the agent of legal improvement which comes after it, in that its claim to authority is grounded, not on the prerogative of any external person or body, not even on that of the magistrate who enunciates it, but on the special nature of its principles, to which it is alleged that all law ought to conform. The very conception of a set of principles, invested with a higher sacredness than those of the original law and demanding application independently of the consent of any external body, belongs to a much more advanced stage of thought than that to which legal fictions originally suggested themselves.

Legislation, the enactments of a legislature which, whether it takes the form of an autocratic prince or of a parliamentary assembly, is the assumed organ of the entire society, and is the last of the ameliorating instrumentalities. It differs from Legal Fictions just as Equity differs from them, and it is also distinguished from Equity, as deriving its authority from an external body or person. Its obligatory force is independent of its principles. The legislature, whatever be the actual restraints imposed on it by public opinion, is in theory empowered to impose what obligations it pleases on the members of the community. There is nothing to prevent its legislating in the wantonness of caprice. Legislation may be dictated by equity, if that last word be used to indicate some standard of right and wrong to which its enactments happen to be adjusted; but then these enactments are indebted for their binding force to the authority of the legislature and not to that of the principles on which the legislature acted; and thus they differ from rules of Equity, in the technical sense of the word, which pretend to a paramount sacredness entitling them at once to the recognition of the courts even without the concurrence of prince or parliamentary assembly. . . .

The Early History of Contract: There are few general propositions concerning the age to which we belong which seem at first sight likely to be received with readier concurrence than the assertion that the society of our day is mainly distinguished from that of preceding generations by the largeness of the sphere which is occupied in it by Contract. Some of the phenomena on which this proposition rests are among those most frequently singled out for notice, for comment, and for eulogy. Not many of us are so unobservant as not to perceive that in innumerable cases where old law fixed a man's social position irreversibly at his birth, modern law allows him to create it for himself by convention; and indeed several of the few exceptions which remain to this rule are constantly denounced with passionate indignation. The point, for instance, which is really debated in the vigorous controversy still carried on upon the subject of negro servitude, is whether the status of the slave does not belong to bygone institutions, and whether the only relation between employer and labourer which commends itself to modern morality be not a relation determined exclusively by contract. The recognition of this difference between past ages and the present enters into the very essence of the most famous contemporary speculations. It is certain that the science of Political Economy, the only department of moral inquiry which has made any considerable progress in our day, would fail to correspond with the facts of life if it were not true that Imperative Law had abandoned the largest part of the field which it once occupied, and had left men to settle rules of conduct for themselves with a liberty never allowed to them till recently. The bias indeed of most persons trained in political economy is to consider the general truth on which their science reposes as entitled to become universal, and, when they apply it as an art, their efforts are ordinarily directed to enlarging the province of Contract and to curtailing that of Imperative Law, except so far as law is necessary to enforce the performance of Contracts. The impulse given by thinkers who are under the influence of these ideas is beginning to be very strongly felt in the Western world. Legislation has nearly confessed its inability to keep pace with the activity of man in discovery, in invention, and in the manipulation of accumulated wealth; and the law even of the least advanced communities tends more and more to become a mere surface-stratum having under it an ever-changing assemblage of contractual rules with which it rarely interferes except to compel compliance with a few fundamental principles or unless it be called in to punish the violation of good faith.

Social inquiries, so far as they depend on the consideration of legal phenomena, are in so backward a condition that we need not be surprised at not finding these truths recognised in the commonplaces which pass current concerning the progress of society. These commonplaces answer much more to our prejudices than to our convictions. The strong disinclination of most men to regard morality as advancing seems to be especially powerful when the virtues on which Contract depends are in question, and many of us have almost instinctive reluctance to admitting that good faith and trust in our fellows are more widely diffused than of old, or that there is anything in contemporary manners which parallels the loyalty of the antique world. From time to time, these prepossessions are greatly strengthened by the spectacle of frauds, unheard of before the period at which they were observed, and astonishing from their complication as well as shocking from criminality. But the very character of these frauds shows clearly that, before they became possible, the moral obligations of which they are the breach must have been more than proportionately developed. It is the confidence reposed and deserved by the many which affords facilities for the bad faith of the few, so that, if colossal examples of dishonesty occur, there is no surer conclusion than that scrupulous honesty is displayed in the average of the transactions which, in the particular case, have supplied the delinquent with his opportunity. If we insist on reading the history of morality as reflected in jurisprudence, by turning our eyes not on the law of Contract but on the law of Crime, we must be careful that we read it aright. The only form of dishonesty treated of in the most ancient Roman law is Theft. At the moment at which I write, the newest chapter in the English criminal law is one which attempts to prescribe punishment for the frauds of Trustees. The proper inference from this contrast is not that the primitive Romans practised a higher morality than ourselves. We should rather say that, in the interval between their days and ours, morality has advanced from a very rude to a highly refined conception—from viewing the rights of property as exclusively sacred, to looking upon the rights growing out of the mere unilateral reposal of confidence as entitled to the protection of the penal law. . . .

In the intercourse of life the commonest and most important of all the contracts are unquestionably the four styled Consensual. The larger part of the collective existence of every community is consumed in transactions of buying and selling, of letting and hiring, of alliances between men for purposes of business, of delegation of business from one man to another; and this is no doubt the consideration which led the Romans, as it has led most societies, to relieve these transactions from technical incumbrance, to abstain as much as possible from clogging the most efficient springs of social movement. Such motives were not of course confined to Rome, and the commerce of the Romans with their neighbours must have given them abundant opportunities for observing that the contracts before us tended everywhere to become Consensual, obligatory on the mere signification of mutual assent. . . .

The Consensual Contracts, it will be observed, were extremely limited in number. But it cannot be doubted that they constituted the stage in the history of Contract-law from which all modern conceptions of contract took their start. The motion of the will which constitutes agreement was now completely insulated, and became the subject of separate contemplation; forms were entirely eliminated from the notion of contract, and external acts were only regarded as symbols of the internal act of volition. The Consensual Contracts had, moreover, been classed in the *Jus Gentium* ["Law of Nations" or "International Law"], and it was not long before this classification drew with it the inference that they were the species of agreement which represented the engagements approved of by Nature and included in her code. This point once reached, we are prepared for several celebrated doctrines and distinctions of the Roman lawyers. One of them is the distinction between Natural and Civil Obligations. When a person of full intellectual maturity had deliberately bound himself by an engagement, he was said to be under a natural obligation, even though he had omitted some necessary formality, and even though through some technical impediment he was devoid of the formal capacity for making a valid contract. The law (and this is what the distinction implies) would not enforce the obligation, but it did not absolutely refuse to recognise it; and natural obligations differed in many respects from obligations which were merely null and void, more particularly in the circumstance that they could be civilly confirmed, if the capacity for contract were subsequently acquired. Another very peculiar doctrine of the *juris consults* could not have had its origin earlier than the period at which the Convention was severed from the technical ingredients of Contract. They taught that though nothing but a Contract could be the foundation of an action, a mere Pact or Convention could be the basis of a plea. It followed from this, that though nobody could sue upon an agreement which he had not taken the precaution to mature into a Contract by complying with the proper forms, nevertheless a claim arising out of a valid contract could be rebutted by proving a counter-agreement which had never got beyond the state of a simple convention. An action for the recovery of a debt could be met by showing a mere informal agreement to waive or postpone the payment.

The doctrine just stated indicates the hesitation of the *Prætors* in making their advances towards the greatest of their innovations. Their theory of Natural law must have led them to look with especial favour on the Consensual Contracts and on those Pacts or Conventions of which the Consensual Contracts were only particular instances; but they did not at once venture on extending to all Conventions the liberty of the Consensual Contracts. They took advantage of that special superintendence over procedure which had been confided to them since the first beginnings of Roman law, and, while they still declined to permit a suit to be launched which was not based on a formal contract, they gave full play to their new theory of agreement in directing the ulterior stages of the proceeding. But, when they had proceeded thus far, it was inevitable that they should proceed farther. The revolution of the ancient law of Contract was consummated when the *Prætor* of some one year announced in his Edict that he would grant equitable actions upon Pacts which had never been matured at all into Contracts, provided only that the Pacts in question had been founded on a consideration (*causa*). Pacts of this sort are always enforced under the advanced Roman jurisprudence. The principle is merely the principle of the Consensual Contract carried to its proper consequence; and, in fact, if the technical language of the Romans had been as plastic as their legal theories, these Pacts enforced by the *Prætor* would have been styled new Contracts, new Consensual Contracts. Legal phraseology is, however, the part of the law which is the last to alter, and the Pacts equitably enforced continued to be designated simply *Prætorian* Pacts. It will be remarked that unless there were consideration for the Pact, it would continue *nude* ["unclothed with the Obligation"] so far as the new jurisprudence was concerned; in order to give it effect, it would be necessary to convert it by a stipulation into a Verbal Contract.

The extreme importance of this history of Contract, as a safeguard against almost innumerable delusions, must be my justification for discussing it at so considerable a length. It gives a complete account of the march of ideas from one great landmark of jurisprudence to another. We begin with Nexum, in which a Contract and a Conveyance are blended, and in which the formalities which accompany the agreement are even more important than the agreement itself. From the Nexum we pass to the Stipulation, which is a simplified form of the older ceremonial. The Literal Contract comes next, and here all formalities are waived, if proof of the agreement can be supplied from the rigid observances of a Roman household. In the Real Contract a moral duty is for the first time recognised, and persons who have joined or acquiesced in the partial performance of an engagement are forbidden to repudiate it on account of defects in form. Lastly, the Consensual Contracts emerge, in which the mental attitude of the contractors is solely regarded, and external circumstances have no title to notice except as evidence of the inward undertaking. It is of course uncertain how far this progress of Roman ideas from a gross to a refined conception exemplifies the necessary progress of human thought on the subject of Contract. The Contract-law of all other ancient societies but the Roman is either too scanty to furnish information or else is entirely lost; and modern jurisprudence is so thoroughly leavened with the Roman notions that it furnishes us with no contrasts or parallels from which instruction can be gleaned. From the absence, however, of everything violent, marvellous, or unintelligible in the changes I have described, it may be reasonably believed that the history of ancient Roman Contracts is, up to a certain point, typical of the history of this class of legal conceptions in other ancient societies. But it is only up to a certain point that the progress of Roman law can be taken to represent the progress of other systems of jurisprudence.

Walter Bagehot
1826-1877

Source: *Physics and Politics* (1872)
Selection: "Verifiable Progress Politically Considered"

Introduction: *Walter Bagehot was a British social theorist, journalist, and businessman who specialized in political and economic theory. He was perhaps best known during his short lifetime as the editor of* The Economist—*a news magazine he edited for the last seventeen years of his life—but to sociologists he was influential for his analysis of custom and its role in social life. To still others, Bagehot was much more than even a brilliant sociological and economic analyst—he was a versatile genius, a man whom President Woodrow Wilson referred to as his "master."*

Although Bagehot was raised by a strict Unitarian father and Anglican mother, he attended the irreligious University College, where he received a Bachelor's degree in 1846 and a Master's in 1848. He soon began to write articles for publication, but his father wanted him to be a barrister and his mother wanted him to work in Stuckey's, a private bank founded by her family that employed Walter's father. She got her way, and for nearly a decade Walter's career as a "country banker" allowed him the intellectual space he required to write and observe important events, such as Louis Napoleon's coup d'état, *which Bagehot witnessed firsthand in December 1851.*

Bagehot was comfortable being a societal critic, and soon attained a position at at The Economist, *where his focus was on politics, economics, and related philosophical matters. Shortly thereafter, circumstances led him to assume sole charge of* The Economist's *editorial functions. While there, he also developed a romantic relationship with Eliza Wilson, the eldest daughter of the publication's owner, James Wilson. They married in 1858, remained married until his death, and had no children. Although she frequently complained about frail health, she survived him by forty-four years.*

Among his books, Physics and Politics *is the one of most interest to the development of sociology, and contains the reading below. To write it, Bagehot had to master and apply the rudiments of various theories, including Darwin's theory of evolution. The book contains a well known phrase that became a cliché of social and political conjecture, "the cake of custom;"*

and its subtitle—"thoughts on the application of the principles of 'Natural Selection' and 'Inheritance' to political society"—tells the essence of what we need to know about his objectives. Those ideas led Bagehot to search for the political prerequisites of progress, and he concluded that societies evolved from a "Preliminary Age" to the "Age of Discussion"—a transformation facilitated by "nation-making" and inter-societal "use of conflict." In this transition, Bagehot posited that inherited national characteristics were among the most important determinanants of the disparate development of different states.

In 1877, when Bagehot died following a "chill," Woodrow Wilson provided an apt epitaph, saying, "Occasionally a man is born into the world whose mission it evidently is to clarify the thought of his generation, and to vivify it; to give it speed where it is slow, vision where it is blind, balance where it is out of poise, saving humour where it is dry—and such a man was Walter Bagehot."

*

The progress of MAN requires the co-operation of MEN for its development. That which any one man or any one family could invent for themselves is obviously exceedingly limited. And even if this were not true, isolated progress could never be traced. The rudest sort of cooperative society, the lowest tribe and the feeblest government, is so much stronger than isolated man, that isolated man (if he ever existed in any shape which could be called man) might very easily have ceased to exist. The first principle of the subject is that man can only progress in "co-operative groups;" I might say tribes and nations, but I use the less common word because few people would at once see that tribes and nations ARE co-operative groups, and that it is their being so which makes their value; that unless you can make a strong co-operative bond, your society will be conquered and killed out by some other society which has such a bond; and the second principle is that the members of such a group should be similar enough to one another to co-operate easily and readily together. The co-operation in all such cases depends on a FELT UNION of heart and spirit; and this is only felt when there is a great degree of real likeness in mind and feeling, however that likeness may have been attained.

This needful co-operation and this requisite likeness I believe to have been produced by one of the strongest yokes (as we should think if it were to be re-imposed now) and the most terrible tyrannies ever known among men—the authority of "customary law." In its earlier stage this is no pleasant power—no "rosewater" authority, as Carlyle would have called it—but a stern, incessant, implacable rule. And the rule is often of most childish origin, beginning in a casual superstition or local accident. . . . [B]ut the nature of customary law as we everywhere find it in its earliest stages is that of coarse casual comprehensive usage, beginning, we cannot tell how, deciding, we cannot tell why, but ruling everyone in almost every action with an inflexible grasp.

The necessity of thus forming co-operative groups by fixed customs explains the necessity of isolation in early society. As a matter of fact all great nations have been prepared in privacy and in secret. They have been composed far away from all distraction. Greece, Borne, Judaea were framed each by itself, and the antipathy of each to men of different race and different speech is one of their most marked peculiarities, and quite their strongest common property. And the instinct of early ages is a right guide for the needs of early ages. Intercourse with foreigners then broke down in states the fixed rules which were forming their characters, so as to be a cause of weak fibre of mind, of desultory and unsettled action; the living spectacle of an admitted unbelief destroys the binding authority of religious custom and snaps the social cord.

Thus we see the use of a sort of "preliminary" age in societies, when trade is bad because it prevents the separation of nations, because it infuses distracting ideas among occupied communities, because it brings alien minds to alien shores. And as the trade which we now think of as an incalculable good is in that age a formidable evil and destructive calamity; so war and conquest, which we commonly and justly see to be now evils, are in that age often singular benefits and great advantages. It is only by the competition of customs that bad customs can be eliminated and good customs multiplied. Conquest is the premium given by nature to those national characters which their national customs have made most fit to win in war, and in many most material respects those winning characters are really the best characters. The characters which do win in war are the characters which we should wish to win in war.

Similarly, the best institutions have a natural military advantage over bad institutions. The first great victory of civilisation was the conquest of nations with ill-defined families having legal descent through the mother only, by nations of definite families tracing descent through the father as well as the mother, or through the father only. Such compact families are a much better basis for military discipline than the ill-bound families which indeed seem hardly to be families at all, where "paternity" is, for tribal purposes, an unrecognised idea, and where only the physical fact of "maternity" is thought to be certain enough to be the foundation of law or custom. The nations with a thoroughly compacted family system have "possessed the earth," that is, they have taken all the finest districts in the most competed-for parts; and the nations with loose systems have been merely left to mountain ranges and lonely islands. The family system and that in its highest form has been so exclusively the system of civilisation, that literature hardly recognises any other, and that, if it were not for the living testimony of a great multitude of scattered communities which are "fashioned after the structure of the elder world," we should hardly admit the possibility of something so contrary to all which we have lived amongst, and which we have been used to think of. After such an example of the fragmentary nature of the evidence it is in comparison easy to believe that hundreds of strange institutions may have passed away and have left behind them not only no memorial, but not even a trace or a vestige to help the imagination to figure what they were.

I cannot expand the subject, but in the same way the better religions have had a great physical advantage, if I may say so, over the worse. They have given what I may call a CONFIDENCE IN THE UNIVERSE. The savage subjected to a mean superstition is afraid to walk simply about the world—he cannot do THIS because it is ominous, or he must do THAT because it is lucky, or he cannot do anything at all till the gods have spoken and given him leave to begin. But under the higher religions there is no similar slavery and no similar terror. . . .

The first work of the first ages is to bind men together in the strong bond of a rough, coarse, harsh custom; and the incessant conflict of nations effects this in the best way. Every nation is an hereditary co-operative group bound by a fixed custom; and out of those groups those conquer which have the most binding and most invigorating customs, and these are, as a rough rule, the best customs. The majority of the "groups" which win and conquer are better than the majority of those which fail and perish, and thus the first world grow better and was improved.

This early customary world no doubt continued for ages. The first history delineates great monarchies, each composed of a hundred customary groups, all of which believed themselves to be of enormous antiquity, and all of which must have existed for very many generations. The first historical world is not a new-looking thing but is very ancient, and according to principle it is necessary that it should exist for ages. If human nature was to be gradually improved, each generation must be born better tamed, more calm, more capable of civilisation—in a word, more LEGAL than the one before it, and such inherited improvements are always slow and dubious. Though a few gifted people may advance much, the mass of each generation can improve but very little on the generation which preceded it; and even the slight improvement so gained is liable to be destroyed by some mysterious atavism—some strange recurrence to a primitive past. Long ages of dreary monotony are the first facts in the history of human communities, but those ages were not lost to mankind, for it was then that was formed the comparatively gentle and guidable thing which we now call human nature.

And indeed the greatest difficulty is not in preserving such a world but in ending it. We have brought in the yoke of custom to improve the world, and in the world the custom sticks. In a thousand cases—in the great majority of cases—the progress of mankind has been arrested in this its earliest shape; it has been closely embalmed in a mummy-like imitation of its primitive existence. I have endeavoured to show in what manner, and how slowly, and in how few cases this yoke of custom was removed. It was "government by discussion" which broke the bond of ages and set free the originality of mankind. Then, and then only, the motives which Lord Macaulay counted on to secure the progress of mankind, in fact, begin to work; THEN "the tendency in every man to ameliorate his condition" begins to be important, because then man can alter his condition while before he is pegged down by ancient usage; THEN the tendency in each mechanical art towards perfection begins to have force, because the artist is at last allowed to seek perfection, after having been forced for ages to move in the straight furrow of the old fixed way.

As soon as this great step upwards is once made, all or almost all the higher gifts and graces of humanity have a rapid and a definite effect on "verifiable progress"—on progress in the narrowest, because in the most universally admitted sense of the term. Success in life, then, depends, as we have seen, more than anything else on "animated moderation," on a certain combination of energy of mind and balance of mind, hard to attain and harder to keep. And this subtle excellence is aided by all the finer graces of humanity. It is a matter of common observation that, though often separated, fine taste and fine judgment go very much together, and especially that a man with gross want of taste, though he may act sensibly and correctly for a while, is yet apt to break out, sooner or later, into gross practical error. In metaphysics, probably both taste and judgment involve what is termed "poise of mind," that is the power of true passiveness—the faculty of "waiting" till the stream of impressions, whether those of life or those of art have done all that they have to do, and cut their full type plainly upon the mind. The ill-judging and the untasteful are both over-eager; both move too quick and blur the image. In this way the union between a subtle sense of beauty and a subtle discretion in conduct is a natural one, because it rests on the common possession of a fine power, though, in matter of fact, that union may be often disturbed. A complex sea of forces and passions troubles men in life and action, which in the calmer region of art are hardly to be felt at all. And, therefore, the cultivation of a fine taste tends to promote the function of a fine judgment, which is a main help in the complex world of civilised existence. Just so too the manner in which the more delicate parts of religion daily work in producing that "moderation" which, upon the whole, and as a rule, is essential to long success, defining success even in its most narrow and mundane way, might be worked out in a hundred cases, though it would not suit these pages. Many of the finer intellectual tastes have a similar restraining effect they prevent, or tend to prevent, a greedy voracity after the good things of life, which makes both men and nations in excessive haste to be rich and famous, often makes them do too much and do it ill, and so often leaves them at last without money and without respect.

But there is no need to expand this further. The principle is plain that, though these better and higher graces of humanity are impediments and encumbrances in the early fighting period, yet that in the later era they are among the greatest helps and benefits, and that as soon as governments by discussion have become strong enough to secure a stable existence, and as soon as they have broken the fixed rule of old custom, and have awakened the dormant inventiveness of men, then, for the first time, almost every part of human nature begins to spring forward, and begins to contribute its quota even to the narrowest, even to "verifiable" progress. And this is the true reason of all those panegyrics on liberty which are often so measured in expression but are in essence so true to life and nature. Liberty is the strengthening and developing power—the light and heat of political nature; and when some "Caesarism" exhibits as it sometimes will an originality of mind, it is only because it has managed to make its own the products of past free times or neighbouring free countries; and even that originality is only brief and frail, and after a little while, when tested by a generation or two, in time of need it falls away.

In a complete investigation of all the conditions of "verifiable progress," much else would have to be set out; for example, science has secrets of her own. Nature does not wear her most useful lessons on her sleeve; she only yields her most productive secrets, those which yield the most wealth and the most "fruit," to those who have gone through a long process of preliminary abstraction. To make a person really understand the "laws of motion" is not easy, and to solve even simple problems in abstract dynamics is to most people exceedingly hard. And yet it is on these out-of-the-way investigations, so to speak, that the art of navigation, all physical astronomy, and all the theory of physical movements at least depend. But no nation would beforehand have thought that in so curious a manner such great secrets were to be discovered. And many nations, therefore, which get on the wrong track, may be distanced— supposing there to be no communication by some nation not better than any of them which happens to stumble on the right track. If there were no "Bradshaw" [a guide for travelers] and no one knew the time at which trains started, a man who caught the express would not be a wiser or a more business-like man than he who missed it, and yet he would arrive whole hours sooner at the capital both are going to. And unless I misread the matter, such was often the case with early knowledge. At any rate before a complete theory of "verifiable progress" could be made, it would have to be settled whether this is so or not, and the conditions of the development of physical science would have to be fully stated; obviously you cannot explain the development of human comfort unless you know the way in which men learn and discover comfortable things. Then again, for a complete discussion, whether of progress or degradation, a whole course of analysis is necessary as to the effect of natural agencies on man, and of change in those agencies. But upon these I cannot touch; the only way to solve these great problems is to take them separately. I only profess to explain what seem to me the political prerequisites of progress, and especially of early progress. I do this the rather because the subject is insufficiently examined, so that even if my views are found to be faulty, the discussion upon them may bring out others which are truer and better.

Ludwig Gumplowicz
1838-1909

Source: *The Outlines of Sociology* (1899)
Selection: "Concept, Function, Scope and Importance of Sociology" and
"The State"

Introduction: *Ludwig Gumplowicz was a sociologist and legal philosopher born in the Republic of Kraków (now in Poland). Being the son of Jewish parents, he became very interested in the suppression of ethnic and minority groups early in his life. As a young man, he studied at the universities of Kraków and Vienna, and then was appointed professor of public law at the University of Graz, in 1875. It was through his writings, however, that he became a major influence on the development of sociology, helping to define the discipline, In particular, Gumplowicz presented a theory about the origin of the state, an institution he claimed resulted from inevitable conflict rather than through cooperation or divine inspiration. Because of the prominent role of conflict in human affairs, he also argued that social progress is neither inevitable nor permanent.*

According to Gumplowicz, although human beings have always had a natural inclination to form groups and develop a feeling of unity—a process he termed "syngenism"— conflict arose early in our history between prepolitical racial groups, and the groups that were victorious formed states. The states developed to become an amalgam of victor and vanquished, and then entered into war with other states. This process of conquest and assimilation, which is universal, recurs on a larger scale until each state finally creates, through coercion, a system of division of labor that results in the formation of social classes. Class struggles ensue, and through such struggles laws are determined by the victors rather than by any notion of abstract justice. Modern civilizations, therefore, result from warfare. Because of this unavoidable process, Gumplowicz could not believe that social planning and welfare measures would be able to save societies from ultimate collapse.

In keeping with his theoretical stance, Gumplowicz felt the autonomous individual has minimal importance in societal affairs, since individuals function only as members of groups, and groups determine individuals' behaviors. As a result, he saw the dynamic of history and social change as being entirely the products of social groups—a view analogous to how one would see conflicts among other species in the biological struggle for existence and growth. Through his analytical lens, Gumpowicz also saw human history as developing cyclically, not linearly, from birth, to growth, to maturation, to decline, to death, before a new cycle begins.

Gumplowicz's viewpoint and theory strongly influenced leading sociologists of the time, such as Gustav Ratzenhofer, Albion W. Small, and Franz Oppenheimer. One of his major works, The Outlines of Sociology, *contains the following discussions of the nature and role of sociology and the theory of the state.*

*

The function of sociology consists in showing that universal laws apply to social phenomena; in pointing out the peculiar effects produced by them in the social domain, and finally in formulating the special social laws.

As we have to deal with social phenomena exclusively in what follows, we must get a clear idea of what they are; we must distinguish the domain of social phenomena from every other; we must explore it and learn the most important groups upon it. In so doing we shall come in contact with the special sciences which are occupied with the special groups and which are very properly designated the "social sciences" in general.

By social phenomena we mean the phenomena which appear through the operation of groups and aggregates of men on one another. The aggregates are the social elements. We must assume that the simplest and the original social elements were primitive hordes, of which, for reasons that have been explained elsewhere, there must have been a great number in remote antiquity.

The combinations of the simple social elements into greater associations—tribes, communities, peoples, states and nations—are just so many social phenomena. There are also psychosocial phenomena, such as language, customs, rights, religion, etc., arising from the action of social elements with or upon the individual mind.

The province of sociology embraces them all. Sociology must investigate them and show the social laws of their development. Many groups, it is true, have been isolated and made the subject-matter of independent sciences. But that should not hinder sociology from subjecting them to a new examination from the standpoint of social science, especially since they have generally been studied from an individualistic standpoint. Sociology should make their social origin and development perfectly clear.

It has just been said that mankind is the substratum of all social phenomena, hence, it is the real subject-matter of sociology. But it is clear that the character of the science will be determined ultimately by our conception of the natural history of mankind. According as our conception is correct or false will sociology be a success or a failure. The smallest mistake in the beginning will avenge itself in hundred and thousand fold greater errors in the end.

Hitherto a very gross misconception has prevailed in social science concerning the natural history of mankind. The character of human phenomena has been completely falsified by conceiving mankind to be genealogically a unitary genus, by supposing lineal descent from a common stock, and explaining varieties of race and type as successive offshoots from it. This fundamental notion set the whole social science on the wrong track. Not only were all right points of view, resulting from the fact of original plurality and variety of races, lost from consideration, but many false ones were presented which produced nothing but errors.

Closely connected with this, indeed resulting from it, is another error. It was conceived that culture and social relations generally, whether of mankind or of particular peoples, develop spontaneously as a plant or animal develops. It was conceived that one and the same group passed through different stages of culture, from the hunting stage to the pastoral, to the agricultural, to warrior life and so on down to industrialism by simple transitions in virtue of an inner law and tendency to develop. But the law of persistence applies to social groups as much as it does to anything else in nature. Social groups persist in their actual social condition and cannot be made to "pass" into another without adequate social cause.

Therefore, we must remember not only that contiguous groups are diverse in origin, but also that they have been undergoing different courses of development. We must also remember that every social group persists in a given condition until forced out of it and into another through the action of some other group, and such action is pre-eminently called social.

In other words, each alteration in the social condition of a group must always have a sufficient social cause, which is always the influence of another group. This is a law, and can be amply illustrated from history and experience. An important proposition for the methodology of sociology follows from it, *viz.*, whenever an alteration in the condition of a group is perceived we should inquire what influences exerted by another group produced it. It follows, also, that a rapid and varied development and frequent social changes occur only under the continual reciprocal influence of many foreign (heterogen) groups, that is, in states and systems of states.

This brings us very close to the definition of a social event or process. When two or more distinct (heterogen) groups come in contact, when each enters the sphere of the other's operations, a social process always ensues. So long as one unitary, homogeneous group is not influenced by or does not exert an influence upon another it persists in the original primitive state. Hence, in distant quarters of the globe, shut off from the world, we find hordes in a state as primitive, probably, as that of their forefathers a million years ago. Here, very likely, we are dealing with an elementary, primitive, social phenomenon or, better, with a social element, but not with a social process nor with social change.

But as soon as one group is exposed to the influence of another, the interplay of mutual forces ensues inevitably and the social process begins. When two distinct (heterogen) groups come together, the natural tendency of each is to exploit the other, to use the most general expression. This, indeed, is what gives the first impulse to the social process. This tendency is so inherent in every human group, so natural and indomitable, that it is impossible to conceive of groups coming together without displaying it, without generating the social process.

The course of the process depends upon the natural constitution of "mankind" and the tendencies peculiar to all human hordes and social communities. Since these factors differ only as one individual or, at most, one species from another and everywhere exhibit the same generic characteristics the process is essentially the same everywhere.

True, the human race is composed of an endless variety of species, the different hordes and tribes are combined in many ways and produce a variety of social formations or collective entities which in turn act upon one another; even the influence of time and place yields a diversity of effects: so that the social process nevertheless presents endless variety and individuality of development. But the differences are transient and local. It is the task of sociology—and by no means an easy one—in the midst of diversity to find the controlling social laws, to explain the miscellaneous variety of social development by the simplest forces in operation and to reduce the countless shapes it assumes to a simple common denominator.

All social laws, indeed all universal laws as well, have one characteristic in common: they explain the becoming, but never the beginning of things, the ultimate origin. This limitation must be insisted upon the more emphatically since the human mind is given to inquiring after the genesis of things. It desires knowledge of the first arising, the ultimate origin—a tendency fatal to science; whereas with all the laws cognizable it can apprehend only the perpetual becoming.

Hence none of the questions about the ultimate origin of human associations belong in sociology, if indeed they belong in any science whatever! Sociology begins with the countless different social groups of which, as can be irrefutably proven, mankind is constituted. The question how they came to be does not belong within its forum.

As we begin by limiting sociological discussion to the becoming of things, excluding discussion of ultimate origin, may we be allowed to point out that the discoveries which are recognized as the greatest achievements of science all lie in the same field. The Copernican discovery applies only to the motion of the planets in their orbits, without inquiring how they came to exist. Harvey discovered the circulation of the blood, a process continually going on under our observation. And we certainly do the great Englishman no wrong in expressing the opinion that when, centuries later, the problem of the "origin of man" shall have long since been laid aside, his investigation into the laws of the becoming, into the "struggle for existence," "adaptation" and "heredity," must still be lauded as an imperishable service to science.

We are unwilling to close this section without emphasizing the importance of the knowledge of social laws to historians and statesmen.

The view that history can be raised to the level of a science only by taking account of the natural and social laws of development is still violently opposed though the reasons for it have been presented many times. We could cite innumerable examples to show how very much history has suffered from ignorance of social laws on the part of the most eminent historians. The most common error, one into which almost every historian has fallen, especially if he is treating of a single nation, is to regard the phenomena as peculiar to one people; whereas did he know social laws he would recognize that they are more general. . . .

Important as sociology is for historians, its significance in politics is greater still. For though hitherto politics has not been reckoned a science at all sociology will give it a scientific character.

At present politics is strife after power. Each state, party and faction, every man even, is striving after power with all the means at command. Material means are supplemented with as cogent reasons as possible. Such reasons and arguments are called the theory of politics. But where is the criterion of their correctness? From the standpoint of success, when the fact has been accomplished, the policy which succeeded is recognized as right. Yet it is not so much ideas and arguments as greater might that makes the project prosperous. So ultimately, greater might is the better policy—as things stand now.

Sociology must give quite another turn to politics; though, indeed, it will develop political science rather than practical politics. That is to say, the social laws which sociology is to formulate from its observations on the processes of history include also the laws of the development of political life. When they shall have been correctly formulated from the past, they must be verified in the present and the future. They must control the course of political development now and hereafter as unequivocally as they have hitherto. But when reliable laws have been formulated, political machinations, tavern politics and ignorant gossip will give place to political foresight and sober calculation based upon positive sociological knowledge.

These words will provoke a sceptical smile—and certainly not without some reason. Similar promises have often proved to be vain talk if not charlatanry even; and usually people who talk of calculating future politics scientifically are not taken seriously, Did not Auguste Comte speak of a *politique positive*, a positive science of politics, which, "instead of pronouncing absolute judgment and suggesting ameliorations," should rather create "a body of scientific conceptions such as has never been outlined nor even suspected by any philosopher before?" Yet how many false and erroneous notions he held! . . .

In one point, however, the old sociologists were clearly right. With presentient mind they suspected the existence of social laws and asserted the possibility of a social science. It is true they did not pass the point of conjecture. They never advanced the true principles of the science, much less to a knowledge of social laws. Nay! They did not even find the starting point of the way which leads to the principles. The point of departure is polygenism. The way is the investigation of the natural relations of distinct (heterogen) groups of men to one another. . . .

Being the science of human society and social laws, sociology is obviously the basis of all the special sciences treating of parts of human society, or of particular manifestations of associative life. Anthropology, the science of man as an individual being, falls within the scope of the universal science of society as a species within the genus. So do ethnography, embracing the description and comparison of existing tribes and peoples; political science, the science of the state treating of social communities which are the result of disciplinary organization; comparative linguistics, or philology; the comparative study of religion, rights, art, etc.—sciences of social institutions which satisfy the psycho-social wants of man; finally political economy and other sciences treating of institutions which the material wants of man as a social unit have produced. It is perfectly natural that all these sciences should have taken shape long before the science in which they should afterward find their basis. This is the normal course of man's developing knowledge.

It was so in natural science in the narrow sense of the word. Botany, zoology and mineralogy took shape before geology and paleontology, though the latter are the foundation of the former. Similarly the art of healing is earlier than physiology.

The explanation is very simple. Things, institutions, relations encountered in concrete form are the first objects observed and investigated. The most convenient hypothesis or crudest explanation suffices for a time to account for their origin. For instance we live under laws constituting a body of rights. The nature of the phenomenon is investigated, the rights are explained, interpreted, compared with others; and their history is traced out. But provisionally their source and origin was satisfactorily explained by saying that the lawgiver proclaimed them. Similarly the explanation of the origin of religion is that God revealed it to His prophet, the founder.

With the progress of knowledge and reflection, ideas concerning the origin of the subjects-matter of the respective sciences undergo changes. The new conclusions come in conflict with the earlier explanations. Thus the comparative study of law showed that rights arise historically in the collective or "folk" mind; and religion, similarly studied, was found to emanate from exigencies of man's spiritual nature, and so on.

Moreover as knowledge broadened the germs of all the psycho-social institutions were eventually found to be in close proximity to one another and the different social sciences met on a common ground—though the common designation was not at once applied. The subject-matter of each science in turn was discovered existing in every people in a greater or less degree, and in a more or less forward state of development. Consequently men were forced to regard the differences in psycho-social phenomena among various peoples and to compare psycho-social products.

The first step was the comparative study of law, especially of customary law, then of religion, language, art and philosophy. This prompted and aided investigation of the common ground whence the fountains of all the sciences seemed to spring. This common ground was at first designated history of civilization, ethnography, or ethnology, Bastian's term. But in fact it may most suitably be called social science.

It discloses the true source of all those psycho-social products that had previously become subject-matter of special sciences. But it does this only because it comprehends the substance of human. Hence we must recognize in sociology the philosophical basis of all the sciences claiming to be "social;" and it will fall to the lot of sociology to demonstrate the relation of each of them to their common basis, and their connection with each other upon it. . . .

The State: The state is a social phenomenon consisting of social elements behaving according to social laws. The first step is the subjection of one social group by another and the establishment of sovereignty; and the sovereign body is always the less numerous. But numerical inferiority is supplemented by mental superiority and greater military discipline. There is a double life in the state; we can clearly distinguish the activities of the state as a whole, as a single social structure, from those emanating from the social elements.

The activities of the state as a whole originate in the sovereign class which acts with the assistance or with the compulsory acquiescence of the subject class. The movement is from within out; it is directed against other states and social groups. Its object is always defence against attacks, increase of power and territory, that is, conquest in one form or another; and its motive, in the ultimate analysis, lies in human providence, in the impulse to secure conditions favorable for existence. The activities within the state are seen in the several social elements and arise naturally from the positions which they occupy in the state and to each other.

The motive of each is essentially the same as that which animates the state as a whole. They seek conditions favorable to existence and therefore endeavor to increase their power. In particular, the superior class seeks to make the most productive use of the subject classes; as a rule this leads to oppression and can always be considered as exploitation. The subject classes strive for greater powers of resistance in order to lessen their dependence.

These are the simplest and most fundamental efforts and they account for the internal and external development of the state, while differences in the history of different states are due to different local and ethnical conditions. As the commonest things of life are often the most difficult to understand, so it is that political scientists to this day have no clear conception of the state; each has his own definition and scarcely one is correct. . . .

If nothing but the universal and essential characteristics of every state were incorporated into the definition, an agreement could be easily reached for there are but two. First, there are certain institutions directed to securing the sovereignty of some over the others; secondly, the sovereignty is always exercised by a minority. A state, therefore, is the organized control of the minority over the majority. This is the only true and universal definition; it is apt in every case.

But many definitions of the state predicate its end, declaring it to be a union or community for securing the common weal, for realizing justice, etc. All this is wholly inadmissible. No state was ever founded with one of these ends in view; and there are many which are states though they have never exhibited even a trace of such a purpose. The truth is that in the course of time under favorable conditions every sovereign organization necessarily acts in harmony with these ends; thus any state may serve them, indeed after reaching a certain stage of development every state does endeavor to advance justice, welfare, etc. But the definition must not be confined to states at one stage of development only; it must apply regardless of the stage which has been or ever will be attained. Moreover, the affirmation of such ends conceals the fact that the single object in organizing a state was to establish the sovereignty of some over the others, and that the results which necessarily followed were not foreseen, much less intended; they cannot be referred to the intention of the founders who followed their own immediate advantage, as all men do. High above egoistic human efforts social development is the product of natural law. . . .

Let us now examine more closely the nature of political relations. Universally there is a ruling minority and a subject majority, this is the essence of the state as it is the essence of sovereignty.

But what is the ruling minority disposed to do? There is but one thing it can wish, *viz.*: to live in better circumstances with the services of the subject majority than it could without them. The result is a common industrial enterprise conducted under compulsion in which the greater burden, all the unfree service, falls upon the subject class though the rulers freely contribute their no less valuable share in support of the political community. Thus compulsory labor is organized through the organization of sovereignty and the whole body of rights.

The kind of industrial labor depends upon the nature of the soil, the climate and the material resources of the state. If the subjected population was roving over rich agricultural lands it will be compelled to till the soil and the conquerors will settle among them so as to exploit both land and people to the best advantage. The agricultural states of Europe still bear traces of such a compulsory organization of labor wherever an exclusive nobility has settled among a numerous agricultural population, spreading itself like a net over the whole land.

But a huge swarm inhabiting an extended prairie and pasture land will adopt a different social organization. The captives taken on many a plundering raid will be distributed among the members to perform the heavier work of tending cattle, transporting tents and the like. The nomadic state thus organized will fulfill its political functions as truly as the settled state of the large property owners. In the latter case the lord upon his manor or in his castle manages the peasants and vassals settled about him, satisfying their simple necessities from the produce of the fields and reserving the surplus for himself. In the nomadic state the master from his chieftain's tent rules over his numerous following, who tend his herds and enjoy a simple subsistence out of the increase; the rest of which, after the richer subsistence of his family is deducted, is added to his accumulated wealth and capital

The organization will be different still where a narrow strip of coast like Phoenicia, or a group of islands like Venice, make agricultural or pastoral pursuits impossible. The superior speculative talent of the ruling class must suggest another method of utilizing the services of the subject class; they will be put to ship-building and employed as sailors, so that the rulers may seek distant coasts and win wealth and power in navigation and foreign trade.

Labor must always be organized under compulsion, the training and the discipline of the state are necessary. It demands of the laboring class, in the beginning at least, untold sacrifice of life and health; but finally in a rising civilization they become participants in the material and moral possessions.

The life of the state is summed up in this common though unequal labor. In it the state performs its task and fulfills its mission, if task and mission can be spoken of where blind impulse rules on every hand; out of it comes the highest moral possession of mankind, civilization.

Gustav Ratzenhofer
1842-1904

Source: *Sociology* (1907)
Selection: "Introduction"

Introduction: *Gustav Ratzenhofer was an Austrian sociologist, military jurist, and soldier. After terminating his formal education before completing secondary school, he tried his hand in the family business of clock making, but soon left that endeavor, at age 17, to become a cadet in the Austrian Army, where he rose to field marshal. His military affiliation remained with him throughout his life, and culminated when he served as president of the supreme military court in Vienna, from 1898 to 1901. It was during his youth, however, as as a cadet, that he apparently developed his interest in sociology, as well as in philosophy and political science, and went on to make major contributions to the social sciences.*

In his influential sociological writings, Ratzenhofer applied Darwin's biological theory of the struggle for existence and "survival of the fittest" to human society. He thus conceived of society, most fundamentally, as an arena of conflicting ethnic and racial groups, and for this reason he is considered a "Social Darwinist." He was also concerned, however, with the development of types of human association, and—despite his conflict approach to society—thought sociology could guide the human species into higher forms of association.

As a Social Darwinist who held an evolutionary viewpoint, Ratzenhofer naturally theorized that large social groups evolved from smaller, less complex social units, and that the evolution took place through conflict. Reducing society to three types of phenomena—chemical, physical, and biological—he held that people's basic drives are rooted in their biological nature. Every person, he claimed, tended to act according to basic drives that include self-preservation (such as the rivalry for food, "Brotneid") and sex (or the "blood bond," "Blutliebe"). Because every human being acts in accordance with these basic drives and interests, the interaction of humans is characterized by a state of "absolute hostility," which is the source of all group conflict.

According to Ratzenhofer, the group conflict usually resulted in one horde conquering another, which eventually led to the formation of a state and the exploitation of the defeated—a condition upon which economic and other social activity was based. Absolute control by a particular state over its subjects was limited, however, by subsequent commercial activities and cultural contacts between states. Over time these limiting processes resulted in "civilization," characterized by "equitable sharing" between and among individuals in the diverse conditions of life.

Ratzenhofer was not only a pioneer in conflict theory but also in socio-political analysis. Around the turn of the twentieth century, his writings had a considerable influence not only on many European social scientists but also on American sociologists, especially Albion W. Small. Among his best known books are the three-volume Wesen und Zweck der Politik (The Character and Purpose of Politics, *1893*), Die Sociologische Erkenntnis (Sociological Perception, *1898*), Positive Ethik (The Positive Ethic, *1901*), Die Kritik des Intellekts (Critique of the Intellect, *1902*), *and* Soziologie (Sociology, *1907*), *which contains the following discussion about the nature of sociology and how it differs from disciplines such as philosophy, anthropology, and history.*

*

By the side of that science which deals with individuals stands on equal footing the science of the reciprocal relationships of human beings. Such is their connection that neither individual nor social life, each treated by itself, can be understood. That biology and psychology, as sciences of the sensible and intellectual occurrences in the life of individual men, have had the start of sociology, as science of the reciprocal relationships of human beings, and that the latter is only now coming to have a secure foundation, although from the beginning social relationships have been inseparable from individual life, is explained by the fact that it is human nature to take itself as the center of the All, and that it is difficult to reach scientific comprehension of social interrelations. Today it has become a certainty that psychology and sociology can thrive only in the most intimate correlation, corresponding with the causal correlation between individual and social life. Both sciences derive their thought-element, however, from philosophy, which should be the synthesis of all human insight.

Because the reciprocal relationships of human beings are an utterly distinct scientific territory, although they are in correlation with all other scientific territories, they constitute a distinct philosophical problem, namely the sociological, which remains unsolved, even if we presume that the cosmological, the psychological, the mathematical, and the logical problems are closed. The social relationships of men, or properly of all organisms, are in a word subject to a regularity which is immediately contained in no other order of regularity, but pertains to this order of relationships as an added factor. It is the task of epistemology (*Erkenntnistheorie*) to make out the causality of all problems, and to determine the relationships of the different orders of regularity in the realms of the cosmic, the physical, the organic, and the social.

Philosophical insight into the origin of the reciprocal relationships of human beings, into the essence of the social forces, and into the regularity of their operation, constitutes, as a portion of positive philosophy, "sociological epistemology" (*sociologische Erkenntnis*). This remains within the boundaries of philosophy.

When, however, research crosses the boundaries of philosophical epistemology, by investigating the biological and psychological elements of social life in the light of their practical facts, the realm of sociology begins. The latter, as science of the reciprocal relationships of human beings, determines the fundamental characteristics of social development, in order to derive from this basis theorems of the ways in which social phenomena may be controlled in the interest of civilization.

Upon its philosophical basis, therefore, sociology will classify the phenomena of the reciprocal relationships of human beings, it will search out the factors of social development, and within this process it will try to determine the workings of natural law in general and of sociological law in particular. Sociology is not called to investigate the numberless incidents of social life, but its province is to work over the results of minute investigation of particular types of occurrences, for the purpose of arriving at a unified survey and comprehension of the coherent regularity of all social phenomena.

Sociology must regard the aggregate of human knowledge as the source of its insight, from which to derive those facts and theorems which correspond with the above purpose. Sociology can consequently not make its way into the microcosm of phenomena. It must devote itself to the total of the same, on pain of never performing its task.

Gustav Ratzenhofer

Because it is the genius of modern science everywhere to press after the particulars, and because, thanks to Hegel's premature fantasies, it has been regarded as beneath the dignity of science to search for the great correlations, the few attempts that have been made to compose sociology in its full circumference have not obtained high repute. On that account some investigators who were in search of a sociology betook themselves to special provinces of social development, and thus became uninvited competitors in every possible branch of knowledge, particularly in national economy, criminal psychology, race psychology, demography, etc. Because there has been as yet no official psychology, while the demand for a science of social relationships was not to be disregarded, many, especially German scholars, presently developed, on the other hand, out of their special fields, sociological researches. Thus history was sociologically pursued (e. g., Lindner, Lamprecht); also economics (Wagner, Schmoller, Sombart); geography (Ratzel); psychology (Wundt); and other sciences. Of course the result of these researches was not raised to the full value of a sociology. In a word, sociology was not able to differentiate itself from its auxiliary sciences.

It is evident that history, the branch of knowledge which assumes the task of making out social phenomena, their genesis, and their consequences, is a principal source of sociological theorems. Indeed in the case of history we have to do with that division of knowledge which up to the present time has regarded itself as called and competent to comprehend instructively the reciprocal relations of human beings as philosophy of history. This vocation has, to be sure, proved to be in vain, because the history lacks the essence of science. Yet history furnishes the bulk of the material for making out the social process. The finest fruit of competent historiography is the support which sociology finds in it for the erection of its system. At bottom the true goal of historiography is sociology. Whatever falls outside of this purpose belongs in the realm of art and of ideals. In spite of the high significance of historical knowledge for sociology, the natural sciences are its foundation, especially those which aim at knowledge of human beings. In this connection biology is the proper source of scientific intelligence, and with it anthropology and ethnology, as next in importance; then history of civilization and statistics as auxiliary sciences at once associate themselves. Geology, paleontology, and geography must always be looked to as advisers. Over this wide realm of the scientific founding of sociological thinking, philosophy (*sociologische Erkenntnis*) must as it were keep watch, in order that the vast unity of all natural evolution may never be lost from sight. Sociology therefore has no limited field of research, like the social sciences, whose theoretical structure gains in certainty in the degree in which the investigator sticks to his specialty. It rather demands categorically the most comprehensive thinking and knowledge. Everything in the sociological field which is capable of specialization into a technology belongs no longer in sociology in the narrower sense, but to the application of its theorems, and this principally affects the theory of politics.

Sociology is not, like most branches of knowledge, a distinct portion of our insight, but in correspondence with its object it extends over our whole knowledge. In the social relationships all the efforts of our intellect flow together, to permit man and his groupings to gain a share in the achievements and purposes of all thinking. The social relationships are not a species of phenomenon in the realm of nature, like the plants or electricity, or in the life-process, like law or religion, but they are human life in itself. Whatever produces, qualifies, impels, and destroys us human beings—all this makes up the social relationships, and in social life the deeds of human beings have their last echoes. Hence the science cannot be a specialism (*Fachstudium*) but merely a synthesis of all knowing, like philosophy.

If therefore, on the one hand, from most branches of knowledge something extends over influentially into sociology, on the other hand sociology furnishes the most fundamental impulses for the sciences of law, of the state, and of economics, by means of which these may at last become true sciences, and have thoroughly purposeful effects.

The need of a comprehensive insight into the reciprocal relationships of human beings becomes more imperative as social complexity increases. Although it remains a duty of specializing science, indefatigably to work for intelligence about the depths of being and becoming, it is not less the duty of synthesizing science to make these results profitable. It is constantly becoming more evident that science cannot possibly accomplish its utmost, if it merely strives for the minute, and dissolves itself in subdivisions. We are coming to see rather that this tendency can be only an auxiliary phenomenon in intellectual development, because all creative work has its conclusion not in unraveling but in combining.

The division of labor is, and always will be, merely a technical trick. All completeness in art and science has its roots in unification.

No one thinks more pessimistically about the final value of all research than the specialist who is always seeing new gaps in his object. He is consequently not qualified to appraise the synthetic purposes of sociology. The sociologist, supported by philosophy, must know when the possibility of a fruit-bearing synthesis is present. This turning-point of an adequate mass of scientific preliminary knowledge appears to have arrived since the complete opening-up of the surface of the earth, and the beginning of world-commerce. Through these facts the highest and last object of sociology, so to speak, the social universe, has presented itself to view. To investigate its laws is the order of the day.

Attainment of the proposed end seems to me to be assured through positive monism as *Weltanschauung*, and through monistic positivism as heuristic method. Monism presents all being to us as the work of a unitary principle of all phenomena, and incidentally society as subject to the inclusive regularity of nature. In this method resides the guarantee, however, that sociology will never lose itself in unproved assertions; that in directions in which special research has reached only negative results, sociology will abstain from dogmatic conclusion, so that, without surrendering the universal purpose of a sociology, the necessary increments and interpretations will have to be reserved for the future.

Vilfredo Pareto
1848-1923

Source: *The Mind and Society* (1916)
Selection: "The Scientific Approach"

Introduction: *Vilfredo Pareto was born in Paris to a French mother and an Italian father, who was a hydrological engineer exiled from his native Genoa because of his political views. After growing up with middle class advantages, Pareto moved to Italy to complete his education in mathematics and literature. At the age of 21, upon graduating from the Polytechnic Institute in Turin, he worked as an engineer for the railroads, where he applied his extraordinary mathematical abilities. In 1889, he married a Russian woman, Dina Bakunin, but they divorced twelve years later. Soon thereafter he married Jane Régis and they remained together throughout the remainder of his life.*

Although he was well informed on economic policy and often debated it, Pareto did not study economics seriously until he was forty-two. A year later, in 1893, he became chair of economics at the University of Lausanne, succeeding his mentor Leon Walras. In 1896, at the age of 49, he had his first authored book published: Cours d'Économie Politique (Course of Political Economy). *In economics, Pareto is best known for the concept named after him—"Pareto optimality"—which refers to the an optimal allocation of resources achieved when it is not possible to make anyone better off without making someone else worse off. Throughout his life, he was an active critic of the Italian government's economic policies, and he published pamphlets and articles denouncing protectionism and militarism, which he viewed as the two greatest enemies of liberty.*

In his later years, Pareto shifted his intellectual focus from economics to sociology, in response to his change of belief about human motivation and behavior, and he spent those years collecting the material for his best-known work, Trattato di Sociologia Generale *(1916), generally translated as* The Mind and Society. *His final work was* Compendio di Sociologia Generale *(1920). In these works, he seems to have turned to sociology for an understanding of why his abstract mathematical economic theories did not work out in practice, in the belief that unforeseen or uncontrollable social factors intervened.*

Vilfredo Pareto

Pareto came to believe that even though people pretend to be acting logically, much social action is nonlogical and much personal action is designed to give spurious logicality to non-rational actions. We are driven, he believed, by what he called certain "residues" and "derivations" from these residues. He claimed that the more important of these have to do with either conservatism or risk-taking among the ruling elite—sentiments that alternate in terms of their dominance at different points in time and define human history. For example, a strong conservative elite with a "lion" mentality gradually changes over to the philosophy of the "foxes" or speculators, until a catastrophe results, and there is a return to conservatism, etc. In his Trattato di Sociologia Generale, *he notably developed the notion of the "circulation of elites," the first social cycle theory in sociology.*

Pareto's sociology was introduced to the United States by George Homans and Lawrence J. Henderson at Harvard, and had considerable influence on many sociologists, especially Talcott Parsons. The following excerpt from The Mind and Society *shows how Pareto defined the growing discipline of sociology, placed it within a scientific framework, discussed the nature of sociological (and other) types of theory, and distinguished between logical-rational and illogical-irrational thinking.*

*

1. Human society is the subject of many researches. Some of them constitute specialised disciplines: law, political economy, political history, the history of religions, and the like. Others have not yet been distinguished by special names. To the synthesis of them all, which aims at studying human society in general, we may give the name of *sociology*.

2. That definition is very inadequate. It may perhaps be improved upon—but not much; for, after all, of none of the sciences, not even of the several mathematical sciences, have we strict definitions. Nor can we have. Only for purposes of convenience do we divide the subject-matter of our knowledge into various parts, and such divisions are artificial and change in course of time. Who can mark the boundaries between chemistry and physics, or between physics and mechanics? And what are we to do with thermodynamics? If we locate that science in physics, it will fit not badly there; if we put it with mechanics, it will not seem out of place; if we prefer to make a separate science of it, no one surely can find fault with us. Instead of wasting time trying to discover the best classification

for it, it will be the wiser part to examine the facts with which it deals. Let us put names aside and consider things.

In the same way, we have something better to do than to waste our time deciding whether sociology is or is not an independent science—whether it is anything but the "philosophy of history" under a different name; or to debate at any great length the methods to be followed in the study of sociology. Let us keep to our quest for the relationships between social facts, and people may then give to that inquiry any name they please. And let knowledge of such relationships be obtained by any method that will serve. We are interested in the end, and much less or not at all interested in the means by which we attain it.

3. In considering the definition of sociology just above we found it necessary to hint at one or two norms that we intend to follow in these volumes. We might do the same in other connections as occasion arises. On the other hand, we might very well set forth our norms once and for all. Each of those procedures has its merits and its defects. Here we prefer to follow the second.

4. The principles that a writer chooses to follow may be put forward in two different ways. He may, in the first place, ask that his principles be accepted as demonstrated truths. If they are so accepted, all their logical implications must also be regarded as proved. On the other hand, he may state his principles as mere indications of one course that may be followed among the many possible. In that case any logical implication which they may contain is in no sense demonstrated in the concrete, but is merely hypothetical—hypothetical in the same manner and to the same degree as the premises from which it has been derived. It will therefore often be necessary to abstain from drawing such inferences: the deductive aspects of the subject will be ignored, and relationships be inferred from the facts directly. . . .

5. Profiting by such experience, we are here setting out to apply to the study of sociology the methods that have proved so useful in the other sciences. We do not posit any dogma as a premise to our research; and our statement of principles serves merely as an indication of that course, among the many courses that might be chosen, which we elect to follow. Therefore anyone who joins us along such a course by no means renounces his right to follow some other. From the first pages of a treatise on geometry it is the part of the mathematician to make clear

whether he is expounding the geometry Of Euclid, or, let us say, the geometry of Lobachevski. But that is just a hint; and if he goes on and expounds the geometry of Lobachevski, it does not follow that he rejects all other geometries. In that sense and in no other should the statement of principles which we are here making be taken.

6. Hitherto sociology has nearly always been expounded dogmatically. Let us not be deceived by the word "positive" that Comte foisted upon his philosophy. His sociology is as dogmatic as Bossuet's *Discourse on Universal History*. It is a case of two different religions, but of religions nevertheless; and religions of the same sort are to be seen in the writings of Spencer, De Greef, Letourneau, and numberless other authors.

Faith by its very nature is exclusive. If one believes oneself possessed of the absolute truth, one cannot admit that there are any other truths in the world. So the enthusiastic Christian and the pugnacious free-thinker are, and have to be, equally intolerant. For the believer there is but one good course; all others are bad. The Mohammedan will not take oath upon the Gospels, nor the Christian upon the Koran. But those who have no faith whatever will take their oath upon either Koran or Gospels—or, as a favour to our humanitarians, on the Social Contract of Rousseau. . . . We are by no means asserting that sociologies derived from certain dogmatic principles are useless; just as we in no sense deny utility to the geometries of Lobachevski or Riemann. We simply ask of such sociologies that they use premises and reasonings which are as clear and exact as possible. "Humanitarian" sociologies we have to satiety— they are about the only ones that are being published nowadays. Of metaphysical sociologies (with which are to be classed all positive and humanitarian sociologies) we suffer no dearth. Christian, Catholic, and similar sociologies we have to some small extent. Without disparagement of any of those estimable sociologies, we here venture to expound a sociology that is purely experimental, after the fashion of chemistry, physics, and other such sciences. In all that follows, therefore, we intend to take only experience and observation as our guides. So far as experience is not contrasted with observation, we shall, for love of brevity, refer to experience alone. When we say that a thing is attested "by experience," the reader must add "and by observation." When we speak of "experimental sciences," the reader must supply the adjective "observational," and so on.

7. Current in any given group of people are a number of propositions, descriptive, preceptive, or otherwise. For example: "Youth lacks discretion." "Covet not thy neighbour's goods, nor thy neighbour's wife." "Love thy neighbour as thyself." "Learn to save if you would not one day be in need." Such propositions, combined by logical or pseudological nexuses and amplified with factual narrations of various sorts, constitute theories, theologies, cosmogonies, systems of metaphysics, and so on. Viewed from the outside without regard to any intrinsic merit with which they may be credited by faith, all such propositions and theories are experimental facts and as experimental facts we are here obliged to consider and examine them.

8. That examination is very useful to sociology; for the image of social activity is stamped on the majority of such propositions and theories, and often it is through them alone that we manage to gain some knowledge of the forces which are at work in society—that is, of the tendencies and inclinations of human beings. For that reason we shall study them at great length in the course of these volumes. Propositions and theories have to be classified at the very outset, for classification is a first step that is almost indispensable if one would have an adequate grasp of any great number of differing objects. To avoid endless repetition of the words "proposition" and "theory," we shall for the moment use only the latter term; but whatever we say of "theories" should be taken as applying also to "propositions," barring specification to the contrary.

9. For the man who lets himself be guided chiefly by sentiment, for the believer, that is, there are usually but two classes of theories: there are theories that are *true* and theories that are *false*. The terms "true" and "false" are left vaguely defined. They are felt rather than explained.

10. Oftentimes three further axioms are present:

(1) The axiom that every "honest" man, every "intelligent" human being, *must* accept "true" propositions and reject "false" ones. The person who fails to do so is either not honest or not rational. Theories, it follows, have an absolute character, independent of the minds that produce or accept them.

(2) The axiom that every proposition which is "true" is also "beneficial," and *vice versa*. When, accordingly, a theory has been shown to be true, the study of it is complete, and it is useless to inquire whether it be beneficial or detrimental.

(3) At any rate, it is inadmissible that a theory may be beneficial to certain classes of society and detrimental to others—yet that is an axiom of modern currency, and many people deny it without, however, daring to voice that opinion.

11. Were we to meet those assertions with contrary ones, we too would be reasoning *a priori*; and, experimentally, both sets of assertions would have the same value—zero. If we would remain within the realm of experience, we need simply determine first of all whether the terms used in the assertions correspond to some experimental reality, and then whether the assertions are or are not corroborated by experimental facts. But in order to do that, we are obliged to admit the possibility of both a positive and a negative answer; for it is evident that if we bar one of those two possibilities *a priori*, we shall be giving a solution likewise *a priori* to the problem we have set ourselves, instead of leaving the solution of it to experience as we proposed doing.

12. Let us try therefore to classify theories, using the method we would use were we classifying insects, plants, or rocks. We perceive at once that a theory is not a homogeneous entity, such as the "element" known to chemistry. A theory, rather, is like a rock, which is made up of a number of elements. In a theory one may detect descriptive elements, axiomatic assertions, and functionings of certain entities, now concrete, now abstract, now real, now imaginary; and all such things may be said to constitute the *matter* of the theory. But there are other things in a theory: there are logical or pseudo-logical arguments, appeals to sentiment, "feelings," traces of religious and ethical beliefs, and so on; and such things may be thought of as constituting the instrumentalities whereby the "matter" mentioned above is utilised in order to rear the structure that we call a theory. Here, already, is one aspect under which theories may be considered. It is sufficient for the moment to have called attention to it.

Albion W. Small
1854-1926

Source: *General Sociology* (1905)
Selection: "The Subject Matter of Sociology"

Introduction: *Albion Woodbury Small was an American sociologist born and raised in Maine. Although he studied theology from 1876 to 1879, at the Andover Newton Theological School, he did more than any other American sociologist to establish sociology as an academic subject; and he shared the leading role, along with Lester F. Ward and Franklin H. Giddings, in defining the scope and status of sociology among the social sciences.*

From 1879 to 1881, Small studied history, economics, and politics at the University of Leipzig and the University of Berlin; and from 1888 to 1889 he studied history at the Johns Hopkins University in Baltimore, MD, from which he received a Ph.D. At the same time he also taught at Colby College, and eventually served as Colby's president from 1889-1892. During those years, Small was especially influenced by welfare economists and sociologist Lester Ward, which led him to view sociology as a discipline that could promote sound social planning and develop a reliable body of secular social ethics.

Among Small's many major accomplishments, in 1892 he founded the first Department of Sociology in the United States, at the University of Chicago, and chaired the department for over thirty years, assembling such sociological luminaries as W. I. Thomas, Robert E. Park, and Ernest W. Burgess. In 1894 he cauthored (with George E. Vincent) the first textbook in sociology: An Introduction to the Study of Society. *In 1895 he established the* American Journal of Sociology, *which he edited for the next thirty years; and in 1905 he helped establish the American Sociological Society and served as its president from 1912 to 1913.*

Small may ultimately be remembered for his lifelong campaign to establish sociology as a valid academic discipline, and for his effort to define the subject matter of sociology and distinguish it from other social science and humanitarian disciplines. In particular, he stressed social process and the associational aspects of human social life as the unique subject matter of sociology. Influenced by theorists who stressed conflict in human affairs, such as Marx, Gumplowicz, Sombart, and Veblen, Small saw the raw material of the social process in group activities, which he believed were based on elemental human interests that resulted in inevitable conflict. Given Small's intellectual influences, it is little wonder that he offered a vigorous critique of the capitalist system. He ultimately believed, however, that anarchy could be prevented if group clashes were carried out under the supervision of the state, with its legitimate authority to arbitrate conflicts.

Small's familiarity with the various social sciences led him to become interested in promoting their synthesis, towards the latter part of his life. For a long time, he had tried to fuse his views with those of Gustav Ratzenhofer, and that effort is clearly evident in his textbook General Sociology *(1905). The following excerpt from that work shows how Small discusses the dynamic role of the conflict of interests, defines the scope and objectives of sociology, outlines the main subdivisions of the field, and states its fundamental ethical goals.*

*

The Subject Matter of Sociology: The proposition to be developed in this chapter, and then in greater detail throughout the syllabus, is that the *subject-matter of sociology is the process of human association.*

Ever since Comte proposed the name " sociology," and parallel with all subsequent attempts to give the term a definite content, one mode of attack upon the proposed science has been denial that it could have a subject-matter not already pre-empted by other sciences. This sort of attack has been encouraged by the seemingly hopeless disagreement among sociologists about the scientific task that they were trying to perform. If sociology has had anything to say about primitive peoples, for instance, it has been accused of violating the territory of anthropology and ethnology. If it has dealt with evidence recorded by civilized races, it has been charged with invading the province of the historian. If it has touched upon the relations of social classes in modern times, the political scientist or the economist has warned it to cease infringing upon his monopoly. Thus sociology has seemed to workers in other sciences either a pseudo-science, attempting to get prestige in their own fields by exploiting quack methods, or a mere collector of the waste thrown aside by the more important sciences. Sociologists themselves have unintentionally done not a little to confirm this impression. As has been hinted above, their failure to agree upon a definition of their science, or upon precise description of their task, has seemed to afford ocular proof that their alleged science was merely a name with no corresponding content.

Has sociology a material of its own? Jealous friends of the older sciences promptly answer "No." Friends of the new science as confidently answer "Yes;" but they have not always been able to justify the answer to each other, or even to themselves.

The formula adopted above is not an individual variation of the many alternatives already proposed as a fair field for a science of sociology. It is rather an interpretation of all the efforts, both within and without the older sciences, which have been prompted by a more or less distinct feeling that there are important reaches of knowledge about human conditions not provided for in the programs of the older sciences. Instead of leading to the conclusion that there is nothing to do which the older sciences do not properly attempt, if the heterogeneous labors of the sociologists are reviewed with a little care they furnish abundant evidence, both that there is unoccupied territory, and that these unsystematized surveys have each actually been doing some of the necessary work of plotting the ground.

The proposition which we are now supporting is not that the sociologists ought to fix upon a new material as the subject-matter of their science. In fact, the sociologists have long ago instinctively fixed upon their material, and its peculiar character is gradually beginning to appear. The subject-matter upon which the sociologists are engaged is the social process as a whole. This is to be sharply distinguished, on the one hand, from mere knowledge of isolated phenomena, or classes of phenomena, that take place among men; and it is also to be distinguished from mere knowledge of immediate relations that may be abstracted from the whole complex of relations which make up the entire fabric of human life. The former kind of knowledge is description, narrative, story, tradition, that does not rise to the generality of science. The latter kind of knowledge may be organized into science of a certain order of generality. This has occurred, schematically at least, in the case of the accepted social sciences—ethnology, history, economics, etc. The sociologists are attempting to develop a general science which will have relations to the special social sciences analogous with the relations of general physics to the special physical sciences, on the one hand, and to the various physical technologies, on the other; or analogous with the relations of general chemistry to subdivisions of chemistry, or the relations of general biology to subordinate sections of biology.

Comparisons of this sort are so loose that they might easily prejudice the case under discussion. They are merely illustrations, necessarily inexact, but presenting certain instructive parallels. Let us suppose that, at a certain stage in the development of the science of physics, investigators had acquired considerable amounts of knowledge about groups of physical phenomena determined by relatively superficial marks. Let us suppose that one type of physicists had specialized upon gravitation, with the least possible attention to all other phases of physical phenomena. Suppose another type had in the same way confined attention to the phenomena of light; another, to those of magnetism; etc. Suppose that in each case the knowledge gained by such abstraction had been carefully systematized. This whole body of knowledge would doubtless have had a certain value. Obviously that value would have been narrowly limited, however, because such arbitrary isolation of things that are essentially related is possible only so long as insight into the real facts is rudimentary. Modern physics could not come into existence until, by some means or other, students of these things had learned to entertain the idea of the unity of their phenomena, resting in an underlying unity of substance manifesting the phenomena.

That is, there could be only superficial arrangements of amateurish observation, not respectable science, until a unifying conception gave coherence to the details observed. Thus the conception of matter, and of the molar and molecular processes of matter, might have arisen after a long history of such unconcerted specialization as we have supposed. These conceptions would presently serve as bonds of connection between the scattered workers. They would serve as clues to common interests between them. They would lead to meanings previously undiscovered in the phenomena, and they would promote further investigation of the phenomena. Thus, in place of desultory pursuit of knowledge about interesting physical facts, there would arise a science of physics. Although the actual development of physics has not literally followed this order, the essential development has involved virtually the above stages. Consciousness of a subject-matter, on the one hand manifesting diverse phenomena, and on the other hand strictly delimited from other subject-matter, has been a precondition of a science of physics at once comprehensive and independent.

We may vary the form of the illustration in the case of chemistry. Suppose something like our present knowledge of chemical occurrences had grown up before there was any such generalization as "matter" or "atomic phenomena." Suppose some men had by some sort of intuition grouped the metals together, and had observed their behavior under different circumstances. Suppose others had studied salts, others acids, etc. Again we should have had a certain grade of knowledge, in a certain system of arrangement; in it we should have had no science of chemistry. There must first have arisen a conception of an order of phenomena common to all matter, and conforming to laws varying merely in details according to the composition and circumstances of the particular portions of matter in question. Otherwise more or less interesting information about capriciously distinguished sorts of matter could never attain the dignity of a science of chemistry.

The like is true of biology, and the literal history of biology has perhaps more obviously conformed to the logical necessity we are citing than the history of physics or chemistry. The "natural history" still found in many schools harks back to conceptions of the organic world which are logically neither more nor less respectable than the traditional English farmer's division of the animal kingdom into "game, vermin, and stock." No matter how patiently one type of men studies plants, and another reptiles, and another fishes, and another birds, and another beasts, and so on, neither one nor all of them could go much beyond advertising the need of a biological science which did not exist. In order that dilettantish natural history might pass over into positive biology, it was necessary that all observation of living nature should submit to control by an antecedent conception of organic matter and laws of the variation of its phenomena.

In a word, whatever the chronological order of occurrence of the ideas, all the concrete and special knowledge that goes to make up our present sciences has been unified at last around some central conception of subject-matter and appropriate method. We may express the fact for our present purposes in the formula: Physics is the science of matter in its molar and molecular processes; chemistry is the science of matter in its atomic processes; biology is the science of matter in its organic processes. In each case the comprehensive science has the task of organizing details which may already have been studied separately by several varieties of scholars.

The same logical methods which have arrived at these generalizations make irresistibly toward the conviction that coherence and unity of knowledge about human experience demand a *science of men in their associational processes*. Many of these processes have long been studied in detail, but study of them in their correlations is, as in the case of chemical and vital processes, the work of a distinct order of science, with a peculiar object of attention. To the range of generalization which the needed general science comprehends in the present case, the men who have most felt the need apply the name *sociology*.

Without referring to details which might further guard this summary comparison, our present interest is in the fact to be illustrated in the case of sociology. The phenomena presented by human beings have been studied in ways which are on the same logical plane with the treatment of organic phenomena by the obsolete types of "natural history." Not to mention the lesser social sciences, conventional history and economics and ethics, as represented by still extant types of thinkers, are sometimes as fragmentary and unvital and uncentered as a "science" of garden vegetables or of draft-horses would be, if not correlated with larger knowledge. The sociologists represent a protest against this situation. The protest has been long in developing out of the spontaneous, inarticulate stage. It is rapidly finding its voice. The formula which we are emphasizing expresses the implicit assumption of all the sociologists who are to be taken seriously. If they could, they would materially weaken the force of the names used to designate the conventional divisions of sciences pertaining to man. The past and present convenience of these names, and of the academic classifications for which they stand, is counterbalanced by the obstructions which they oppose to the progress of real knowledge. They interfere with discovery that all serious students of society are investigating phases of the same subject-matter. The supreme need in the human sciences at the present moment is to make out what that one subject-matter is, and how the different kinds of research are related to it. This central and comprehensive reality appears to the sociologists as *the associational process*.

Albion W. Small

Wherever there are human beings there are phenomena of association. Those phenomena constitute a process composed of processes. There can be no convincing science of human life till these processes arc known, from least to greatest, in the relation of each to each and to all. Knowledge of human life which stops short of this is at best a fragment, and at worst a fiction. Hence we assert that studies of selected phases of human affairs, no matter how ancient and awful the tradition that sponsors them, are logically in the class of pseudo-sciences, until they take their place within the plexus of sciences which together interpret the whole process of human association.

Men who call themselves by either of the names that signify attachment to either of the traditional divisions of knowledge are at liberty to define their intellectual interests for themselves, and to shape their individual pursuits accordingly. Thus certain interests may posit a "science" of archaeology; others, a "science" of epigraphy; others, a "science" of cartography; others, a "science" of numismatology; and so on, up to history, and law, and economics, and cosmic philosophy. Men of each type may cultivate their peculiar section of knowledge as though it outranked every other kind of knowledge. Not group-provincialisms, however, but the reality of objective relations, must determine at last whether a selected portion of knowledge is relatively a fragment or a whole, relatively insignificant or important. No incident, phase, machinery, institution, product, stage, or program of human life is central enough to clothe knowledge of it with more than the rank of a tributary science. The process that is taking place among men, through the ages and across the ages, is the largest whole of which men can have positive knowledge. This whole consequently fixes the goal of complete science of human life. No less than this whole is contemplated by the sociologist as his aim. He necessarily represents a desired generalization of knowledge which is farther than any other scientific program from actual or probable completion. Sociology thus defined is, and must remain, more a determining point of view than a finished body of knowledge. At the same time, and by virtue of both these sides of its case, sociology exposes the relativity and the partialness of any body of knowledge which comprehends less than the full sweep of the social process. Whatever be the appraisal of the fractional sciences in the subjective estimate of their promoters, the objective importance of each of them is measured by the kind and amount of tribute it can bring to knowledge of the human process as a whole.

These conceptions have been expressed in such general terms that repetition in less abstract form may not be superfluous. Wherever two or more human beings are within each other's ken, there is set up between them action and reaction, exchange of influence of some sort or other. That influence, on the one hand, molds the individuals concerned, tending to make, unmake, remake them without end; and, on the other hand, it composes those individuals into more or less rigid group-relationships, perhaps after having decomposed previous relationships to another group. This reciprocating process, growing infinitely complex as the circle of association widens, and as the type of individual becomes more and more evolved—including, besides its form, the content of the process, first in the evolving objective conditions within which the association takes place, second in the developing consciousness of the persons engaged in the process—this is the human reality, and all knowledge of human conditions is abortive in the degree in which it fails to fill out a complete expression of this reality.

Let us suppose the savage man A, and the savage woman B, of the horde X. Their wants are few. Food is plenty. B supplies it for A, who eats till he is satisfied, and treats his food-getter with tolerable gentleness. But the food grows scarce. The horde breaks up into foraging pairs. A and B wander beyond their usual haunts, and encounter the savage man C of horde Y. They had never met before. To an impartial observer there is little to distinguish the savage A from the savage C. Up to date all the ferocity which we associate with the word "savage" may have been dormant in both. In each other's presence new factors of stimulation and response begin to operate. Each wants food. Each wants the woman. Each wants to eliminate the other. Treating the woman as merely a passive factor, we have in action rudiments of the universal process of association, viz., antithesis of individuals, stimulus of one by the other, through the medium of common or conflicting wants, self-assertion by the opposing individuals, resulting reconstruction of the individuals themselves. That is, they fight; one prevails, and is transformed from a socially indifferent personality into a master; the other yields, and is transformed from a socially indifferent personality into a slave. The group is changed from a diad into a triad. Both A and B, we may suppose, become subject to C, while the relation of neither A nor B to C is precisely identical with the previous relation of A and B to each other.

This process of individual and group-reaction, remaking both the individuals and the groups, extends from the savage group of two or more, to the most comprehensive and complex group of groups which ultimate civilization may develop. It is incessant. It is perpetually varying. It is the main movement, within which migrations, race-mixtures, wars, governments, constitutions, revolutions, reformations, federations, civilizations, are merely the more or less important episodes, or situations, or factors. This whole process is the supreme fact within the reach of human knowledge. It is the final interpreter of each and every lesser fact which may attract human attention. Since this process, from beginning to end, from component to completeness, in its forms and in its forces, in its origins, its variations, and its tendencies, is the subject-matter which sociology proposes to investigate, the relation of every other science to sociology is fixed, not by the dictum of any scientist, but by the relation which the subject-matter and the methods of other sciences bear to knowledge of the entire social process.

To make the point more precise, we may distinguish the work of sociology in turn from that of ethnology, of history, and of economics. Before passing to these specifications, or illustrations, we must provide for all necessary corrections of the personal equation. We will not assume, whether to the advantage or the disadvantage of either science, that any single man, still less a single fragment of his work, fairly represents the whole of his science. We will not even venture to assume that our use of the material to be cited for illustration gives all the credit due to the writer from whom it is taken. His own views of the final correlation of that material with other subjects of knowledge may be quite unobjectionable. Our purpose is merely to illustrate the point that, in the form in which it appears in a given version of one of these sciences, the same objective material may have no interest whatever for sociology, or, on the other hand, it may be viewed in such relations as, at one and the same time, to furnish subject-matter for one of these sciences and also for sociology. To express the case from the point of view of desirability, as I see it, and of ultimate adjustment, as I predict it, there will presently be no apparently statical dualism or multipleism between the subject-matter of the other human sciences and that of sociology;

When every student of human life realizes that the reality which he tries to know is a one, not a many, each will regard the material of his immediate science, not as belonging to his science *instead of* belonging to another science, but as being to some extent the common material of several sciences, or at most as held in trusteeship by his science for its final use in the complete science.

In this spirit we may cite for illustration, first, the little book, Deniker's *The Races of Man*. The author states his purpose as follows: "My object . . . has been to give . . . the essential facts of the twin sciences of anthropology and ethnography" (Preface). In carrying out this purpose a chapter is devoted to each of the following subjects:

"Somatic Characters;" "Morphological Characters;" "Physiological Characters;" "Ethnic Characters;" "Linguistic Characters;" "Sociological Characters" (a chapter each on "Material Life," "Psychic Life," "Family Life," and "Social Life"); "Classification of Races and Peoples;" "Races and Peoples of Europe;" "Races and Peoples of Asia;" "Races and Peoples of Africa;" "Races and Peoples of Oceania;" "Races and Peoples of America."

Without passing judgment upon the expressed or implied correlations in which the author views this material, we may repeat our abstract propositions in terms of the particulars which he schedules. If there be a science or sciences that are content to discover, describe, compare, and classify such details as these, and *therewith to let the matter rest*, such sciences may be credited with a preserve of their own, from which sociology holds itself unconcernedly aloof. With these details, simply as details, or merely as foils reciprocally to display each other as curiosities, sociology has no manner of concern. If the items thus considered are the subject-matter of any science, sociology is not likely to disturb either its possession or its title.

On the other hand, every one of these details has occurred somewhere along in the course of the process in which rudimentary men, and rudimentary human associations, evolve into developed personalities and complex associations. With the whence, and the how, and the why, and the whither of this process, sociology is supremely concerned. If any of the details in question can be brought into such visible relation with this social process, and in the precise measure in which they can be made to shed light upon the process, they come within the scope of sociology.

Thus the most spectacular detail, like a racial peculiarity, or a ceremonial anomaly which remains unaccounted for, may be the chief pride and the center of attraction in an ethnological museum. It would have no value at all for sociology. If, however, it could be made to yield any evidence whatever about the facts, or the forms, or the forces, or the conditions, or the laws of the social process, to just that extent it would come to be the common material of sociology and of the science which exhibits it in the museum.

In the same way we may distinguish between the object of attention in sociology and the subject-matter beyond which certain types of mind do not pry in studying history. . . .

In the modern literature classed as "history" we accordingly find quaint and curious information in all stages of organization, from a minimum to a maximum of coherence. Our argument is that sociology has no part nor lot with the type of history which is content to find out facts *and there rest its case.* Like all genuine science, sociology is not interested in facts as such. It is interested only in relations, meanings, valuations, in which facts reappear in essentials. One fact is worth no more than another, if its correlation with other facts is concealed. On the other hand, every fact in human experience has a value of its own as an index of the social process that emerges in part in the fact. In so far as the historian hunts down facts for the purpose of finding the social process revealed in the facts, his interest is identical with that of the sociologist. The difference between them is again merely a difference of greater or less attention to different steps of one and the same approach to knowledge of the social reality. We might imitate a verbal distinction familiar in a related field, and say that as ethnography is to ethnology, so is *historiography* to *historiology.* I would by no means concede that the subject-matter of sociology is confined to the past. It is still more concerned with interpretation of the social process in the present. This term "historiology" is suggested as a synonym for one segment of the arc of sociology, and merely as a temporary expedient in this particular part of the argument. To point the contrast between mere discovery of details of past experience, and the work that the sociologists want to do, we may fairly call the former historiography and the latter "historiology."

The real progress of the historians toward promotion of science is not in the line of which many of them have recently grown so proud.

History does not become more scientific by shifting its attention from relatively insignificant kings and soldiers to equally insignificant common folks. History becomes scientific in proportion as it advances from knowledge of details toward reconstruction of the whole in which the details have their place. The sociologists have entered the field of social science with a plea for a fair share of attention to that correlation of knowledge, notorious neglect of which has thus far been the paradox of our era of "inductive science."

Recurring to the titles from Stubbs, we may add that investigation of such topics may, and indeed must, proceed in the first instance with severe disregard of collateral details. The test of historical work, however, is not where it begins, but where it ends. It is a misconception of fact, and a misuse of terms, to speak of any program that begins and ends with details as "scientific." Historiography as such is not science; it is merely a technique. The output of that technique is raw material of science. There is no more scientific value in knowing merely that William the Conqueror, or William the Red, or any of their successors in past centuries, did this or that, than there is in knowing what Edward VII and the Kaiser did on their yachts at Kiel last summer. We do not reach science till we advance from knowledge of what occurred to knowledge of the meaning of what occurred. On the side of the meanings of occurrences, whoever follows connections as far as they can be traced, whether he calls himself historian or sociologist, pursues the essential sociological interest. Happily it is impossible for the most atomistically minded historiographer utterly to overlook the pointings of each event or situation toward connections with other events and situations. Even a list of topics like the one we have cited at random testifies of this necessity. "Results," "state," "growth," "policy," "introduction," "maintenance," "transitional," are all terms of relationship. Moreover, the relationships implied are not merely those of nearness in time or space, nor of series. They are relationships of working-with, of process. This process may be contemplated merely within an arbitrarily restricted area; e. g., causes and effects so far as they appear in contrasts between the before and the after of relations of classes, of economic systems, of constitutional principles, of legal enactments, of social customs, of religious conventions, *in a certain population*. In this case there is rudimentary, but narrowly restricted, recognition that specific knowledge gets its value by correlation with other knowledge. The interest of the historian converges toward that of the sociologist in the precise degree in which the former desires to advance from knowledge of occurrences as such, not merely to their immediate correlations. but to their last discoverable meanings as indexes of the whole process of social evolution. At one extreme is sheer interest in bare details. At the other extreme is interest that rates everything short of dynamic interpretation of the details as mere preliminary.

The same distinction may he stated in terms of discrimination between the economic and the sociological interest. Again, it should be urged with all emphasis that every use of words which implies an exclusive division of subject-matter among the social sciences is merely a convenient concession to a condition which the progress of science should at least mitigate. As we have said above, from the sociological viewpoint different workers in the social sciences are not working on different kinds of material. They are merely carrying on different divisions of labor upon one material. That material is human experience in general. Regardless of the special name by which sections of it are known, the total purpose of social science in general, up to the point where it ceases to be mere knowledge and begins to pass over into power, is to discover the meanings of human experience. Our present illustration should bring out another real difference between degrees of approach toward this end. . . .

To the sociologist, every type of individual, every combination of activities, every institution, whether economic, political, artistic, scientific, or religious, is of interest, not for its separate self, but so far as it can shed or reflect light about the articulations and the motivations of the process as a whole, in which each detail in its own degree is an incident. Without involving ourselves in a boundary dispute with the psychologists, we may repeat that the sociological interest begins with individuals feeling wants. How do those wants bring them into contact with other individuals feeling wants? How do the individuals thus in contact modify each other's wants? How do the wants of the separate individuals become a species of environment, conditioning all the individuals? How does the reaction between the elements—i. e., individuals, physical environment, and social environment—become complex, and ever more complex, in the progressively varying reaction of cause and effect within the combination? How do types of want, and of individual and social contact, and of environment, result from the different stages of this process? What significance, at any stage of the process, have details, or groups of details, or systems of details, as means of interpreting the process?

Thus, from the sociological point of view, either a group of economic facts, or the economic system of an age or a civilization, or the economic theory of a culture epoch, is each in its way merely a term in the whole proposition which sociology is trying to formulate. The human interest is in knowing the human whole. The sociologists have broken into the goodly fellowship of the social scientists, and have thus far found themselves frankly unwelcome guests. They have a mission, however, which will not always be unrecognized. Their part in the whole work of knowing the human reality is, in the first place, to counteract the tendency of specialists to follow centrifugal impulses. The tendency has already gone so far that social science is apparently split into fragments which cannot be reorganized into a unified body of knowledge. Sociology stands first for the coordinating stage in the knowing process. Recognition of its legitimacy and its necessity is merely a question of time. We have specified some of the grounds for this belief, in an editorial reviewing the course of thought about sociology during the past decade.

To recapitulate: The sociologists are attempting to show that salvation of the social sciences from sterility must be worked out, not by microscopic description and analysis of details alone, but by such correlation and generalization of particulars that the whole social process will be intelligible. The limits of this chapter restrict discussion to that phase of sociological theory in which intellectual apprehension is uppermost. From the human standpoint no science is an end in itself. The proximate end of all science is organization into action. The ultimate interest of the sociologists, therefore, is in turning knowledge of the social process into more intelligent promotion of the process.

Beatrice Potter Webb

1858-1943

Source: *The Co-Operative Movement in Great Britain* (1904)
Selection: "Conclusions"

Introduction: *Martha Beatrice Potter Webb, an English sociologist, econo-mist, socialist, labor historian, and social reformer, is well known for both her writings and social activism. She is also famous for her literary and social collaborations with her husband, Sidney Webb, who was given the title "Baron Passfield" in 1929 (which thus made Beatrice "Baroness Pass-field"). Along with her husband and others, Webb played a central role in founding both the Fabian Society in 1884—a British socialist organization dedicated to advancing the principles of socialism through gradualist and reformist means—and the London School of Economics and Political Science in 1895. In her many works she coined several well known phrases, perhaps the most famous being "collective bargaining"—a phrase still com-monly used today.*

Webb first became a charity worker to study poverty in Britain, as she was especially concerned with the prevalence of poor people who existed among societal riches. After working among the poor for a while, she devel-oped the notion that in a capitalist society attempts to reform the economic system could be best understood by studying working class groups that were actually implementing alternative economic practices—such as coopera-tives. She subsequently focused on understanding the relationship between the economy, social classes, and the state. This led her to conclude, unlike Karl Marx, that state intervention was necessary to control the economy. As a result, she advocated gradual—rather than revolutionary—change.

Webb self-identified as a "cooperative federalist," which referred to a school of thought that promoted consumers' cooperatives; and she felt that such cooperatives should form cooperative wholesale societies (such as the English Cooperative Wholesale Society) and purchase farms or factories. She thus rejected the notion of "worker cooperatives," which referred to cooperatives that allowed those who did the work and benefitted from it to have some degree of control over how work was done. Although some work-er cooperatives were successful in her time, she felt they failed to usher in the form of socialism she favored, which was led by volunteer committees of people like herself. Despite such feelings, her final book, The Truth about Soviet Russia *(1942) celebrated central planning.*

With the support of the Fabians, Beatrice Webb coauthored many books and pamphlets on socialism and the cooperative movement. In them, she made a number of important contributions to the political and economic theory of the cooperative movement. Among her books are The History of Trade Unionism *(1894),* Industrial Democracy *(1897), and* The Cooperative Movement in Great Britain *(1891), which contains the reading below on the cooperative movement and its relationship to democracy, socialism, interpersonal relationships, trade, and political policy.*

*

I WILL assume, in the remarks with which I propose to end this slight sketch of the British Co-operative Movement, that we, like the early Co-operators, are socialists; that we accept, as the Ideal towards which we are tending, a state of society in which all citizens will serve the community with whole-heartedness, the community remunerating them, in return, according to the personal expenditure needful to the full and free use of their mental and physical faculties. Without this desire for, and faith in, a possible socialist state, these observations will appear uncalled for. I should therefore advise the student who desires only a matter-of-fact statement of past or present events, or the philosopher who is satisfied with society as it at present exists, to close the book, as the few remaining paragraphs will afford him no nutriment, and may even supply an irritant which will effectually prevent the comfortable digestion of the preceding narrative, and of the statistics contained in the Appendix.

Have we citizens of Great Britain then any certain ground for faith or even for hope that through the concurrent action of the Co-operative and trade union organization we shall attain Robert Owen's New System of Society; a state in which the earnings of all workers will represent efficient citizenship, while all citizens will render willing service according to their highest ability? The answer, I fear, is no longer doubtful. Even if Trade Unionists and Co-operators worked in unison, voluntary association, though an admirable training and convincing example, would be found wanting as a sole and all-sufficient method of social reform.

For the Co-operative movement, though a striking and imposing example of a complete solution of the administrative difficulties of an industrial democracy, forms at the present time an altogether insignificant part of the national industry. The total capital of the country is estimated at ten thousand millions. Only twelve millions of this is administered by voluntary associations of consumers. But the enthusiastic Co-operator will ask: why not develop the voluntary system of democratic Co-operation until it embraces the whole field of industry? It may be well, therefore, to inquire briefly into the probable social and economic limits to the further extension of this form of democratic self-government.

The first barrier to an indefinite extension of the Co-operative movement under the present social system are the conditions of life of certain classes. Men living below a certain standard of life, or in isolation, populations continually shifting their abode and changing their occupation, are incapable of voluntary association, whether as consumers or producers. The hand-to-mouth existence of the casual labourer, the physical inertia of the sweater's victim, the vagrant habits and irregular desires of the street hawker, and of the mongrel inhabitants of the common lodging-house—in short, the restlessness or mortal weariness arising from lack of nourishment, tempered by idleness, or intensified by physical exhaustion, do not permit the development, in the individual or the class, of the qualities of democratic association and democratic self-government. We need no demonstration of the truth of this fact; it is the burden of complaint at Trade Union and Co-operative Congresses. Thus, I imagine, it is no mere coincidence that Co-operative and trade union organizations flourish best in state-regulated trades, such as textile and mining industries; while the wage-earners of Birmingham and London, at work in their homes, or in workshops that escape regulation, are apparently incapable of association as consumers or producers. The labour history of the last fifty years tells us plainly that legislative regulation—the outcome of compulsory association—is the only effectual instrument for raising the condition of certain classes to the social plane upon which voluntary association becomes possible. But whether or not we admit that the absence of legislative restriction is the principle cause of this incompetency, it is indisputable that about four-fifths of the wage-earning class are outside the Co-operative and trade union movements.

Poverty and irregular habits form a lower limit to the growth of Co-operation. Fastidiousness and the indifference bred of luxury constitute a higher limit to the desire or capacity for democratic self-government. The upper and middle class, with incomes altogether out of proportion to their actual needs, demand the servility of the profit-making traders and the irregular and diversified production of profit-making manufacturers. The business-like despatch and quick answers of the Store official jar on the sensitive feelings of the great lady, accustomed to the silent sub-servience and immediate acquiescence of well-bred servants, paid to wait on her pleasure and convenience. The caprices of fashion, the vagaries of personal vanity and over-indulged appetites can find no satisfaction in an organization of industry based on the supply of rational and persistent wants. Moreover, the severe mental strain consequent on the consci-entious expenditure of a large income, or the apathy of a mechanical sat-isfaction of every want disinclines the wealthy customer for the respon-sibilities of association. Physical nausea and mental exhaustion are the common ailments of the rich, as well as the complaints of the very poor, while the love of personal possessions, and the spirit of rivalry en-gendered by social ambition, effectually withdraw the surplus energies of the well-to-do classes from any form of democratic association. To bring, therefore, the great bulk of the middle and upper class expenditure within the jurisdiction of the Co-operative movement we should be forced to impose a graduated income-tax amounting to something like twenty shillings in the pound, on all incomes over 400 pounds a year. Propaganda among the rich is as futile as propaganda among the very poor; if the Co-operators "mean business" with those classes of society, they must add certain items to their political programme the character of which there is no need to specify.

The social limits are not the only boundaries of the Co-operative State. The administrative limits are, if anything, more important. For the group of citizens who administer a Store or the Wholesale Society are necessarily the actual consumers of commodities or services supplied through those organizations. Now this special form of democracy does not always form a possible or desirable and administrative group. We cannot imagine the Calais and Dover Line of steamers being owned and managed by the actual passengers. If it were deemed desirable that the community should undertake this service, we should follow the example of the Belgian Government in the service of the Ostend and Dover route, and the central government would provide a national line of steamers. Again, the most ardent Co-operator, who aimed at the communal administration of railways, would hardly contend that the proper administrative group for the London and North Western was the passengers and traders who used it. All persons, whether or no they travel by rail, are indirectly interested in the means of transit as consumers or producers of articles upon which carriage is paid. Hence an important body of consumers would be disfranchised; while the difficulty of gathering together a genuinely and permanently representative body of the different classes of passengers and traders would render a steady and uniform administrative policy impossible. In the single instance of a consumer's organization undertaking the means of transit—the Liverpool Docks—the franchise has been limited to traders paying at least 10 pounds annual dues, so as to form, from out of the casual and scattered constituency of customers, a responsible body of proprietors permanently interested in the good management of the docks. And even on the Mersey Docks Harbour Board the community at large is directly represented by four nominees of the government.

Hence in some of the largest and most important industries an open democracy of consumers forms an undesirable or impossible constituency for representative self-government. But this is by no means the most important administrative limit. In all cases of a national or artificial monopoly the actual consumer is an improper representative of the community. We could not, for instance, endow the farmers and agricultural labourers with the land of the nation; no body of proprietors which excluded any portion of the community would be a satisfactory constituency. If our mineral wealth were to be nationalized, the mines would not be handed over to the colliery proprietors or even to the coal miners. Moreover, when consumption is compulsory, association must also be compulsory. The provision of such articles of universal consumption as water, gas, roads, street-lights, must obviously be undertaken by a compulsory association of consumers, if we desire to maintain an industrial democracy. For instance, if the Sheffield Store had undertaken to raise the two and a half millions recently paid by that municipality for its water-works, it is obvious that the Sheffield Co-operative Society would have become a combination of capitalists making profit or suffering loss by a speculative supply of the wants of those Sheffield citizens who, through ignorance or indifference, remained outside the association. In other words, we should again have returned to the individualist system of industry, with its advantages and disadvantages—a form of society which we are not at present discussing.

And in this example of the Sheffield Store we touch on a financial as well as an administrative limit to the rapid growth of Co-operative compared to other forms of democratic enterprise. While a municipality, through the collective power of compulsory association, can raise millions every year by its assessment on the citizens, the Store accumulates capital at a snail's pace. . . . To sum up, therefore, these obvious limits to the Co-operative commonwealth, we may state that all the larger forms of national wealth, such as land, means of transit, and all commodities of compulsory consumption—gas, water, sanitary appliances, etc.—are excluded from the possible domain of voluntary associations of consumers.

But the statement of the boundaries of the Co-operative State is not yet complete. The whole national export trade is necessarily excluded. . . . It is, of course, conceivable that the Store system might be developed among other Anglo-Saxon nations with whom we trade, and that a relationship such as exists between the Scotch and English Wholesale Societies might be established in the corresponding central establishments of Australasia, Canada, America, and Great Britain. But other forms of socialism seem likely to obtain in Australasia; and the American people, intent on personal gain, show neither desire nor capacity for any form of government other than a nominal democracy ruled by a corrupt plutocracy. On the other hand, the British Stores and Wholesale Societies might frankly engage in a profitable export trade with the merchants of foreign countries; or they might export surplus manufacture, so as to obtain the increasing return from manufacturing on a large scale in those industries in which they are already engaged. But the danger to the integrity and prosperity of the Co-operative movement of this step is easily demonstrated. All the economic advantages of the control of production by the actual consumers are abandoned. Once again Co-operators taste the forbidden fruit of industry—profit on price. Supposing the profit from the export trade became a considerable portion of their total income, voluntary associations of consumers, able at any moment to limit their numbers, would be sorely tempted to close their doors to new-comers. Thus the Wholesale Societies might be transformed into profit-making machines of capitalist producers, and the habit of trading with non-members abroad might be rapidly extended into the custom of trading with non-members at home. With the quotation of the shares of the Stores and the Wholesale Societies on the Stock Exchange, rising and falling in value with the advent of a new directorate, or the rumour of a foreign war, the whole fabric of the Rochdale system [a type of co-operative system] might fall into disrepair, if not into hopeless ruin, by internal competition between societies, or combination among them against the interests of the whole community.

Thus, those of us who believe in the millennium of a fully developed industrial democracy, perceive in the national export trade the last resort of capitalist administration of industry. No mere voluntary association of Co-operators can undertake the export trade. Here again the only possible participation of democratic Co-operation would bring us rapidly back to the individualist system—profit on price for individual gain. Should these industries therefore eventually fall into the hands of the representatives of a democracy, they must obviously be administered by the public organization of the whole people—that is, by the State or the municipality. For in this manner only can the profits, which will necessarily accrue from dealings with other States, be accumulated for the benefit, or distributed for the satisfaction, of the whole body of citizens.

The limits of the probable domain of the Co-operative State are now all within sight. Voluntary associations of consumers are practically restricted to the provision of certain articles of personal use, the production of which is not necessarily a monopoly, the consumption of which is not absolutely compulsory, and for which the demand is large and constant. Under the present social system a restricted portion only of the nation is within reach of a social democracy—that intermediate class neither too poor nor too wealthy for democratic self-government. Let us attempt to reduce these limits to a statistical form in relation to the total income of the United Kingdom. I must however warn the reader that I offer with all reserve the following estimate, with the hypothetical figures upon which it is based. I use these figures as a convenient form of summing up certain arguments, and not as an accurate calculation of the present or future possibilities of the Co-operative movement.

Let us assume that Co-operators, although unwilling to reduce the incomes of the well-to-do classes by legislative measures, were determined to use their political power to level up the standard of life among the degraded classes to the plane of voluntary association. Assuming, moreover, that in this attempt they were successful, the Stores and dependent federal institutions might then hope to attract the whole expenditure of working-class income within their sphere. Of the 1,300 millions of national income, 500 millions, at most, is attributed by statisticians to the wage-earning class. From this let us deduct 100 millions for rent, gas and water rates, and taxes. The commodities or services which these charges represent, we have already shown to be outside any possible extension of the Co-operative system. Another seventy millions of working-class income is spent in alcohol; no Co-operator proposes to undertake the provision of spirits and beer to the Co-operative world. We have therefore a remainder of 300 to 350 millions. Hence this sum might represent the Co-operative trade. But it is needless to remind the reader that the income of the working class, and more especially that proportion of it which could be spent at the Store, is capable of almost indefinite increase. For instance, the "drink bill" would probably be reduced to a modest pittance if all working men developed the qualities of democratic self-government. And without any recourse to socialistic measures, the gross income of the working class might be considerably enlarged. But there is every reason to suppose that the same conditions of increased intelligence and sobriety among the workers would enable capitalists to obtain larger returns and landlords to exact higher rent. In other words, whatever might be the increase of the total wealth of the nation, the proportionate share of the workers in the national income would, other things being equal, remain the same.

The trade of the working-class Stores therefore might, even under the present social circumstances, increase from the present turnover of 35 millions to the 350 millions of working-class income spent in household provisions. Narrower limits are set to Co-operative manufacturing. A very small proportion of these commodities could be produced under the Co-operative system of industry. Imports of food and tobacco constitute the great bulk of the wage- earner's consumption. Of the remainder, we must subtract what is spent, not on new commodities, but on second-hand articles, which have already passed through the hands of the well-to-do classes, of which there is undoubtedly a large working-class consumption. And lastly we are face to face with the economic limit of the unit of productivity—I mean a sufficiently large demand for any one article to allow of profitable manufacture. For instance, the Wholesale Society has hitherto felt itself unable, in spite of the proximity of its chief centre to the great cotton industry, to undertake the manufacture of cotton cloth. The range of variety in calicoes and prints bought by the working class render the quantity of any one quality or style demanded by Co-operators too small for profitable manufacture even by their central institution. This unit of productivity is the blank wall which Co-operators have already discerned as the practical barrier to democratic manufacturing. I need not, however, point out that this barrier to Co-operative manufacture would be pushed further and further by the extension of Co-operative trade.

To sum up this rough estimate, therefore, we can hardly conceive that the Co-operative turnover, under the present social conditions, could exceed 300 to 400 millions—a trade which would only admit of 75 millions of capital, should the present ratio between Co-operative capital and trade be maintained. As the working-class capital is estimated at the present time at 169 millions, we shall therefore always be face to face with the present difficulty of using the capital of the working class in the Stores and the Wholesale Societies. Hence Co-operators are right in asserting that they will always have a superabundance of capital at their command for which the democratic school of Co-operators can find no employment. We may confidently predict therefore, that the individualist school of Co-operators, should I be mistaken in my view of the economic and administrative obstacles to the realization of their ideal of the self-governing workshop, and should they succeed in converting the British working class to their principles, would always have at their disposal a large margin of working-class capital. The custom of the wealthy, anxious to secure quality, and able to pay a good price for a good article, and stimulated to benevolent interest in individualist effort by fear of approaching socialism, might become the happy hunting ground of the self-governing workshop; while the whole export trade might be transferred to industrial partnerships, with their autocratic capitalist administration and profit-sharing wage-system. Thus the various forms of Co-operative enterprise need not compete. The individualist school of

Co-operators, in fact, if they surmount purely economic obstacles, will find that their antagonists are the Trade Unions, and not the officials of the Stores or the directors of the Wholesale Societies.

I have refused to consider one limit to the administrative capacity of the Co-operative organization frequently described by the opponents of the democratic form of Co-operation—the centralized government of the Wholesale Societies. First, because I believe that the constitutional structure of these Federations is indefinitely elastic and adaptable. Secondly, because I imagine that the administration of some seventy-five millions of capital, and the organization of a trade of some 350 millions, though an arduous undertaking, is not beyond the capacity of the present Store system, even if the constitutions of their dependent Federations were to remain unchanged.

These then are the external boundaries to the possible domain of the voluntary associations of consumers. But there are also internal obstacles to the realization of the dream of the enthusiastic Co-operator—the absorption by a Co-operative community of the whole of the tribute now levied on the workers by those who "toil not, neither do they spin." A large portion of the income of the community is paid, not for personal services rendered to the nation, but to capitalists and landlords. Co-operators do not escape the payment of this tax. For, like the Owenite communities actually established, the members of the Store and the Wholesale Societies, surrounded by a competitive system of industry, cannot escape the tribute of rent and interest even within their own domain. Doubtless with regard to the interest on the twelve millions of Co-operative capital, it is credited to associates, that is to say, it is charged on the consumption of all members and paid to a minority of capitalist Co-operators. The rent of land, however, is usually, if not always, levied by an outsider, either in the form of technical rent or as interest on the capital expended in the purchase of the freehold. . . . Hence the Co-operative system of industry has taken only one step forward in completing the work of the industrial revolution foreshadowed by Robert Owen. Through the open democracy of the Store it has exchanged an individualist for a social administration of industry, and thus secured the profits of enterprise for the community at large. This first step, however, is the most difficult. The democratic administration of industry involves the possession of active intellectual and moral qualities; whereas the inhabitants of hospitals and asylums are equal to the passive receipt of rent and interest. But the British Co-operative movement has left the ownership of land and the means of subsistence in the hands of individuals, whether within or without the Co-operative State. If the English democracy therefore wishes to complete the social changes prophetically described in Robert Owen's New System of Society, if they are determined to add to the social production of wealth (brought about by the new industry) and to the communal administration and control (introduced by the Co-operative and trade union movements) the communal ownership of land and the means of production, they must use deliberately the instruments forged by political democracy—taxation in all its forms on unearned wealth and surplus incomes, and compulsory acquisition, not necessarily without personal compensation, of those portions of the national wealth ripe for democratic administration. And we have ample precedent for class taxation, and personal compensation, as a method whereby the democracy may acquire or control the instruments of production. A Conservative government recently proposed to use the drink tax to buy out the publicans; a Radical government might suggest a land tax to buy out the landlords, and doubtless Mr. Ritchie, as Chancellor of the Exchequer in a future Conservative government, will impose a graduated Municipal Death Duty on real property, whereby the dwellings as well as the streets might gradually become the property of the corporation. But, like the details of a reformed Poor Law, these measures of relief to a class overburdened with property are without the scope of an essay on that form of democratic industry known as the Co-operative movement.

In conclusion, I would emphatically re-assert that the social, administrative and economic boundaries of the Co-operative State by no means limit the power of Co-operators in our national life. The gathering together of the whole working class in a Co-operative Union on the one hand, and in a Federation of Trade Unions on the other, would make the workers practically paramount in the State. The organization of workers as consumers would effectually prevent any attempt on the part of capitalists and landlords to bribe certain sections of the working class by the promise of high money wages to support a protectionist policy in its legislative form, import duties, or, in its economic form, trusts and capitalist combinations to raise prices. And if the officials of these twin

Federations, representing the primeval interests of consumption and production, were to unite in solemn compact, then it would be comparatively easy to weed out of the community those who consume without producing, the parasites of all classes; while those who at present produce without consuming their full portion would be raised to a higher place in the national banquet. That this result cannot be accomplished without resort to legislation—the outcome of compulsory association—has, I think, been clearly demonstrated. But before we can have a fully developed democracy, the nation at large must possess those moral characteristics which have enabled Co-operators to introduce democratic self-government into a certain portion of the industry, commerce and finance of the nation. It is, therefore, as moral reformers that Co-operators pre-eminently deserve the place in the vanguard of human progress. While completing and extending their domain to its furthermost limits, Co-operators should deliberately introduce their methods and experience into the administration of the parish, the municipality, the county and the State; thus fulfilling by the sure but slow process of democratic self-government Robert Owen's Co-operative system of industry.

Thus the two distinct bodies of social reformers created by the teaching of Robert Owen—British Co-operators and British Socialists—once again united by a common desire for industrial democracy under the banner of Radical Reform, may accept as a full and complete expression of their aims and methods the noble words of that great democrat John Bright :—"I believe that ignorance and suffering might be lessened to an incalculable extent, and that many an Eden, beauteous in flowers and rich in fruits, might be raised up in the waste wilderness which spreads before us. But no class can do that. The class which has hitherto ruled in this country has failed miserably. It revels in power and wealth, while at its feet, a terrible peril for its future, lies the multitude which it has neglected. If a class has failed, let us try the nation. That is our faith, that is our purpose, that is our cry—let us try the nation."

Jane Addams
1860-1935

Source: *Democracy and Social Ethics* (1902)
Selection: "Filial Relations"

Introduction: *Jane Addams was a pioneer American sociologist, settlement social worker, public philosopher, author, and leader in women's suffrage and world peace. A native of Cedarville, IL, she was the youngest of nine children born into a prosperous family. When she was only four years old, she developed Potts' Disease, which caused a curvature in her spine and lifelong health problems. At age 21, in 1881, she graduated from Rockford Female Seminary, and in 1889 she founded (with Ellen Gates Starr) the world famous social settlement, the Hull House. Located on Chicago's Near West Side, the neighborhood was teaming with newly arrived working-class and poor immigrants from diverse backgrounds: Italian, Irish, German, Greek, Russian, and Jewish, soon followed by African-American and Mexican immigrants. Once the Hull House was established, Addams not only worked but also lived there for most of her life, following the practice of most ardent settlement house workers at that time.*

In addition, she actively supported the campaign for woman suffrage, the founding of the National Association for the Advancement of Colored People (1909), and the American Civil Liberties Union (1920); and during World War I she worked to found the Women's Peace Party, which became the Women's International League for Peace and Freedom (WILPF) in 1919, serving as its first president. As a result of her work, she became the first American woman ever to be awarded the Nobel Peace Prize, in 1931.

While stressing human reason as a path to realizing democratic ideals, Addams also valued our emotional life, especially human kindness and sociability. She held that we need to understand each other's points of view and value relationships over individuality if we are to transform social democracy from a mere political creed to a way of life. In suggesting how to realize these ideals, she promoted several strategies, such as using formal education to educate the public about social democracy and encouraging individuals to act independently of their social class, sex, ethnic, and racial groups.

Addams viewed sociological theory and research as a means to reform society—especially by alleviating social problems brought on or exacer-

bated by the rapidly emerging social changes that were transforming Amer-
ica, such as urbanization, industrialization, immigration, and universal
education. Her concept of the "social ethic" was often a focus of her work,
and refers to individual action based on the welfare of the community in a
democratic society. In her sociological analyses, Addams focused on both
"micro-level" interactions, following the approach of George Simmel and
George Herbert Mead, and on "macro-level" analyses, such as the conflicts
between modern democratic educational institutions and the family. In
particular, she was concerned with the conflicts this caused for young
women, as may be seen in the reading below from Democracy and Social
Ethics, *her earliest book on ethics.*

*

In considering the changes which our increasing democracy is constantly
making upon various relationships, it is impossible to ignore the filial relation. This chapter deals with the relation between parents and their
grown-up daughters, as affording an explicit illustration of the perplexity
and mal-adjustment brought about by the various attempts of young
women to secure a more active share in the community life. We constantly see parents very much disconcerted and perplexed in regard to
their daughters when these daughters undertake work lying quite outside
of traditional and family interests. These parents insist that the girl is carried away by a foolish enthusiasm, that she is in search of a career, that
she is restless and does not know what she wants. They will give any
reason, almost, rather than the recognition of a genuine and dignified
claim. Possibly all this is due to the fact that for so many hundreds of
years women have had no larger interests, no participation in the affairs
lying quite outside personal and family claims. Any attempt that the
individual woman formerly made to subordinate or renounce the family
claim was inevitably construed to mean that she was setting up her own
will against that of her family's for selfish ends. It was concluded that
she could have no motive larger than a desire to serve her family, and her
attempt to break away must therefore be willful and self-indulgent.

The family logically consented to give her up at her marriage, when
she was enlarging the family tie by founding another family. It was easy
to understand that they permitted and even promoted her going to college, travelling in Europe, or any other means of self-improvement, be-

cause these merely meant the development and cultivation of one of its own members. When, however, she responded to her impulse to fulfill the social or democratic claim, she violated every tradition.

The mind of each one of us reaches back to our first struggles as we emerged from self-willed childhood into a recognition of family obligations. We have all gradually learned to respond to them, and yet most of us have had at least fleeting glimpses of what it might be to disregard them and the elemental claim they make upon us. We have yielded at times to the temptation of ignoring them for selfish aims, of considering the individual and not the family convenience, and we remember with shame the self-pity which inevitably followed. But just as we have learned to adjust the personal and family claims, and to find an orderly development impossible without recognition of both, so perhaps we are called upon now to make a second adjustment between the family and the social claim, in which neither shall lose and both be ennobled.

The attempt to bring about a healing compromise in which the two shall be adjusted in proper relation is not an easy one. It is difficult to distinguish between the outward act of him who in following one legitimate claim has been led into the temporary violation of another, and the outward act of him who deliberately renounces a just claim and throws aside all obligation for the sake of his own selfish and individual development. The man, for instance, who deserts his family that he may cultivate an artistic sensibility, or acquire what he considers more fullness of life for himself, must always arouse our contempt. Breaking the marriage tie as Ibsen's "Nora" did, to obtain a larger self-development, or holding to it as George Eliot's "Romola" did, because of the larger claim of the state and society, must always remain two distinct paths. The collision of interests, each of which has a real moral basis and a right to its own place in life, is bound to be more or less tragic. It is the struggle between two claims, the destruction of either of which would bring ruin to the ethical life. Curiously enough, it is almost exactly this contradiction which is the tragedy set forth by the Greek dramatist, who asserted that the gods who watch over the sanctity of the family bond must yield to the higher claims of the gods of the state. The failure to recognize the social claim as legitimate causes the trouble; the suspicion constantly remains that woman's public efforts are merely selfish and captious, and are not directed to the general good. This suspicion will never be dissipated until parents, as well as daughters, feel the democratic impulse and recognize the social claim.

Our democracy is making inroads upon the family, the oldest of human institutions, and a claim is being advanced which in a certain sense is larger than the family claim. The claim of the state in time of war has long been recognized, so that in its name the family has given up sons and husbands and even the fathers of little children. If we can once see the claims of society in any such light, if its misery and need can be made clear and urged as an explicit claim, as the state urges its claims in the time of danger, then for the first time the daughter who desires to minister to that need will be recognized as acting conscientiously. This recognition may easily come first through the emotions, and may be admitted as a response to pity and mercy long before it is formulated and perceived by the intellect. The family as well as the state we are all called upon to maintain as the highest institutions which the race has evolved for its safeguard and protection. But merely to preserve these institutions is not enough. There come periods of reconstruction, during which the task is laid upon a passing generation, to enlarge the function and carry forward the ideal of a long-established institution. There is no doubt that many women, consciously and unconsciously, are struggling with this task. The family, like every other element of human life, is susceptible of progress, and from epoch to epoch its tendencies and aspirations are enlarged, although its duties can never be abrogated and its obligations can never be cancelled. It is impossible to bring about the higher development by any self-assertion or breaking away of the individual will. The new growth in the plant swelling against the sheath, which at the same time imprisons and protects it, must still be the truest type of progress. The family in its entirety must be carried out into the larger life. Its various members together must recognize and acknowledge the validity of the social obligation. When this does not occur we have a most flagrant example of the ill-adjustment and misery arising when an ethical code is applied too rigorously and too conscientiously to conditions which are no longer the same as when the code was instituted, and for which it was never designed. We have all seen parental control and the family claim assert their authority in fields of effort which belong to the adult judgment of the child and pertain to activity quite outside the family life. Probably the distinctively family tragedy of which we all catch glimpses now and then, is the assertion of this authority through all the entanglements of wounded affection and misunderstanding. We see parents and children acting from conscientious motives and with the tenderest affection, yet bringing about a misery which can scarcely be hidden.

Such glimpses remind us of that tragedy enacted centuries ago in Assisi, when the eager young noble cast his very clothing at his father's feet, dramatically renouncing his filial allegiance, and formally subjecting the narrow family claim to the wider and more universal duty. All the conflict of tragedy ensued which might have been averted, had the father recognized the higher claim, and had he been willing to subordinate and adjust his own claim to it. The father considered his son disrespectful and hard-hearted, yet we know St. Francis to have been the most tender and loving of men, responsive to all possible ties, even to those of inanimate nature. We know that by his affections he freed the frozen life of his time. The elements of tragedy lay in the narrowness of the father's mind; in his lack of comprehension and his lack of sympathy with the power which was moving his son, and which was but part of the religious revival which swept Europe from end to end in the early part of the thirteenth century; the same power which built the cathedrals of the North, and produced the saints and sages of the South. But the father's situation was nevertheless genuine; he felt his heart sore and angry, and his dignity covered with disrespect. He could not, indeed, have felt otherwise, unless he had been touched by the fire of the same revival, and lifted out of and away from the contemplation of himself and his narrower claim. It is another proof that the notion of a larger obligation can only come through the response to an enlarged interest in life and in the social movements around us.

The grown-up son has so long been considered a citizen with well-defined duties and a need of "making his way in the world," that the family claim is urged much less strenuously in his case, and as a matter of authority, it ceases gradually to be made at all. In the case of the grown-up daughter, however, who is under no necessity of earning a living, and who has no strong artistic bent, taking her to Paris to study painting or to Germany to study music, the years immediately following her graduation from college are too often filled with a restlessness and unhappiness which might be avoided by a little clear thinking, and by an adaptation of our code of family ethics to modern conditions.

It is always difficult for the family to regard the daughter otherwise than as a family possession. From her babyhood she has been the charm and grace of the household, and it is hard to think of her as an integral part of the social order, hard to believe that she has duties outside of the family, to the state and to society in the larger sense. This assumption that the daughter is solely an inspiration and refinement to the family itself and its own immediate circle, that her delicacy and polish are but outward symbols of her father's protection and prosperity, worked very smoothly for the most part so long as her education was in line with it. When there was absolutely no recognition of the entity of woman's life beyond the family, when the outside claims upon her were still wholly unrecognized, the situation was simple, and the finishing school harmoniously and elegantly answered all requirements. She was fitted to grace the fireside and to add lustre to that social circle which her parents selected for her. But this family assumption has been notably broken into, and educational ideas no longer fit it. Modern education recognizes woman quite apart from family or society claims, and gives her the training which for many years has been deemed successful for highly developing a man's individuality and freeing his powers for independent action. Perplexities often occur when the daughter returns from college and finds that this recognition has been but partially accomplished. When she attempts to act upon the assumption of its accomplishment, she finds herself jarring upon ideals which are so entwined with filial piety, so rooted in the tenderest affections of which the human heart is capable, that both daughter and parents are shocked and startled when they discover what is happening, and they scarcely venture to analyze the situation. The ideal for the education of woman has changed under the pressure of a new claim. The family has responded to the extent of granting the education, but they are jealous of the new claim and assert the family claim as over against it.

The modern woman finds herself educated to recognize a stress of social obligation which her family did not in the least anticipate when they sent her to college. She finds herself, in addition, under an impulse to act her part as a citizen of the world. She accepts her family inheritance with loyalty and affection, but she has entered into a wider inheritance as well, which, for lack of a better phrase, we call the social claim. This claim has been recognized for four years in her training, but after her return from college the family claim is again exclusively and strenuously asserted. The situation has all the discomfort of transition and compromise. The daughter finds a constant and totally unnecessary conflict between the social and the family claims. In most cases the former is repressed and gives way to the family claim, because the latter is concrete and definitely asserted, while the social demand is vague and unformulated. In such instances the girl quietly submits, but she feels wronged whenever she allows her mind to dwell upon the situation. She either hides her hurt, and splendid reserves of enthusiasm and capacity go to waste, or her zeal and emotions are turned inward, and the result is an unhappy woman, whose heart is consumed by vain regrets and desires.

If the college woman is not thus quietly reabsorbed, she is even reproached for her discontent. She is told to be devoted to her family, inspiring and responsive to her social circle, and to give the rest of her time to further self-improvement and enjoyment. She expects to do this, and responds to these claims to the best of her ability, even heroically sometimes. But where is the larger life of which she has dreamed so long? That life which surrounds and completes the individual and family life? She has been taught that it is her duty to share this life, and her highest privilege to extend it. This divergence between her self-centred existence and her best convictions becomes constantly more apparent. But the situation is not even so simple as a conflict between her affections and her intellectual convictions, although even that is tumultuous enough; also the emotional nature is divided against itself. The social claim is a demand upon the emotions as well as upon the intellect, and in ignoring it she represses not only her convictions but lowers her springs of vitality. Her life is full of contradictions. She looks out into the world, longing that some demand be made upon her powers, for they are too untrained to furnish an initiative. When her health gives way under this strain, as it often does, her physician invariably advises a rest. But to be put to bed and fed on milk is not what she requires. What she needs is simple, health-giving activity, which, involving the use of all her faculties, shall be a response to all the claims which she so keenly feels.

Jane Addams

It is quite true that the family often resents her first attempts to be part of a life quite outside their own, because the college woman frequently makes these first attempts most awkwardly; her faculties have not been trained in the line of action. She lacks the ability to apply her knowledge and theories to life itself and to its complicated situations. This is largely the fault of her training and of the one-sidedness of educational methods. The colleges have long been full of the best ethical teaching, insisting that the good of the whole must ultimately be the measure of effort, and that the individual can only secure his own rights as he labors to secure those of others. But while the teaching has included an ever-broadening range of obligation and has insisted upon the recognition of the claims of human brotherhood, the training has been singularly individualistic; it has fostered ambitions for personal distinction, and has trained the faculties almost exclusively in the direction of intellectual accumulation. Doubtless, woman's education is at fault, in that it has failed to recognize certain needs, and has failed to cultivate and guide the larger desires of which all generous young hearts are full.

During the most formative years of life, it gives the young girl no contact with the feebleness of childhood, the pathos of suffering, or the needs of old age. It gathers together crude youth in contact only with each other and with mature men and women who are there for the purpose of their mental direction. The tenderest promptings are bidden to bide their time. This could only be justifiable if a definite outlet were provided when they leave college. Doubtless the need does not differ widely in men and women, but women not absorbed in professional or business life, in the years immediately following college, are baldly brought face to face with the deficiencies of their training. Apparently every obstacle is removed, and the college woman is at last free to begin the active life, for which, during so many years, she has been preparing. But during this so-called preparation, her faculties have been trained solely for accumulation, and she has learned to utterly distrust the finer impulses of her nature, which would naturally have connected her with human interests outside of her family and her own immediate social circle. All through school and college the young soul dreamed of self-sacrifice, of succor to the helpless and of tenderness to the unfortunate. We persistently distrust these desires, and, unless they follow well-defined lines, we repress them with every device of convention and caution. . . .

Fortunately a beginning has been made in another direction, and a few parents have already begun to consider even their little children in relation to society as well as to the family. The young mothers who attend "Child Study" classes have a larger notion of parenthood and expect given characteristics from their children, at certain ages and under certain conditions. They quite calmly watch the various attempts of a child to assert his individuality, which so often takes the form of opposition to the wishes of the family and to the rule of the household. They recognize as acting under the same law of development the little child of three who persistently runs away and pretends not to hear his mother's voice, the boy of ten who violently, although temporarily, resents control of any sort, and the grown-up son who, by an individualized and trained personality, is drawn into pursuits and interests quite alien to those of his family. This attempt to take the parental relation somewhat away from mere personal experience, as well as the increasing tendency of parents to share their children's pursuits and interests, will doubtless finally result in a better understanding of the social obligation. The understanding, which results from identity of interests, would seem to confirm the conviction that in the complicated life of to-day there is no education so admirable as that education which comes from participation in the constant trend of events. There is no doubt that most of the misunderstandings of life are due to partial intelligence, because our experiences have been so unlike that we cannot comprehend each other. The old difficulties incident to the clash of two codes of morals must drop away, as the experiences of various members of the family become larger and more identical. At the present moment, however, many of those difficulties still exist and may be seen all about us. In order to illustrate the situation baldly, and at the same time to put it dramatically, it may be well to take an instance concerning which we have no personal feeling. The tragedy of King Lear has been selected, although we have been accustomed so long to give him our sympathy as the victim of the ingratitude of his two older daughters, and of the apparent coldness of Cordelia, that we have not sufficiently considered the weakness of his fatherhood, revealed by the fact that he should get himself into so entangled and unhappy a relation to all of his children. In our pity for

Lear, we fail to analyze his character. The King on his throne exhibits utter lack of self-control. The King in the storm gives way to the same emotion, in repining over the wickedness of his children, which he formerly exhibited in his indulgent treatment of them.

It might be illuminating to discover wherein he had failed, and why his old age found him roofless in spite of the fact that he strenuously urged the family claim with his whole conscience. At the opening of the drama he sat upon his throne, ready for the enjoyment which an indulgent parent expects when he has given gifts to his children. From the two elder, the responses for the division of his lands were graceful and fitting, but he longed to hear what Cordelia, his youngest and best beloved child, would say. He looked toward her expectantly, but instead of delight and gratitude there was the first dawn of character. Cordelia made the awkward attempt of an untrained soul to be honest and scrupulously to express her inmost feeling. The king was baffled and distressed by this attempt at self-expression. It was new to him that his daughter should be moved by a principle obtained outside himself, which even his imagination could not follow; that she had caught the notion of an existence in which her relation as a daughter played but a part. She was transformed by a dignity which recast her speech and made it self-contained. She found herself in the sweep of a feeling so large that the immediate loss of a kingdom seemed of little consequence to her. Even an act which might be construed as disrespect to her father was justified in her eyes, because she was vainly striving to fill out this larger conception of duty. The test which comes sooner or later to many parents had come to Lear, to maintain the tenderness of the relation between father and child, after that relation had become one between adults, to be content with the responses made by the adult child to the family claim, while at the same time she responded to the claims of the rest of life. The mind of Lear was not big enough for this test; he failed to see anything but the personal slight involved, and the ingratitude alone reached him. It was impossible for him to calmly watch his child developing beyond the stretch of his own mind and sympathy.

That a man should be so absorbed in his own indignation as to fail to apprehend his child's thought, that he should lose his affection in his anger, simply reveals the fact that his own emotions are dearer to him than his sense of paternal obligation. Lear apparently also ignored the common ancestry of Cordelia and himself, and forgot her royal inheritance of magnanimity. He had thought of himself so long as a noble and indulgent father that he had lost the faculty by which he might perceive himself in the wrong. Even in the midst of the storm he declared himself more sinned against than sinning. He could believe any amount of kindness and goodness of himself, but could imagine no fidelity on the part of Cordelia unless she gave him the sign he demanded.

At length he suffered many hardships; his spirit was buffeted and broken; he lost his reason as well as his kingdom; but for the first time his experience was identical with the experience of the men around him, and he came to a larger conception of life. He put himself in the place of "the poor naked wretches," and unexpectedly found healing and comfort. He took poor Tim in his arms from a sheer desire for human contact and animal warmth, a primitive and genuine need, through which he suddenly had a view of the world which he had never had from his throne, and from this moment his heart began to turn toward Cordelia.

In reading the tragedy of King Lear, Cordelia receives a full share of our censure. Her first words are cold, and we are shocked by her lack of tenderness. Why should she ignore her father's need for indulgence, and be unwilling to give him what he so obviously craved? We see in the old king "the over-mastering desire of being beloved, selfish, and yet characteristic of the selfishness of a loving and kindly nature alone." His eagerness produces in us a strange pity for him, and we are impatient that his youngest and best-beloved child cannot feel this, even in the midst of her search for truth and her newly acquired sense of a higher duty. It seems to us a narrow conception that would break thus abruptly with the past and would assume that her father had no part in the new life. We want to remind her "that pity, memory, and faithfulness are natural ties," and surely as much to be prized as is the development of her own soul. We do not admire the Cordelia who through her self-absorption deserts her father, as we later admire the same woman who comes back from France that she may include her father in her happiness and freer life. The first had selfishly taken her salvation for herself alone, and it was not until her conscience had developed in her new life that she was driven back to her father, where she perished, drawn into the cruelty and wrath which had now become objective and tragic.

Historically considered, the relation of Lear to his children was archaic and barbaric, indicating merely the beginning of a family life since developed. His paternal expression was one of domination and indulgence, without the perception of the needs of his children, without any anticipation of their entrance into a wider life, or any belief that they could have a worthy life apart from him. If that rudimentary conception of family life ended in such violent disaster, the fact that we have learned to be more decorous in our conduct does not demonstrate that by following the same line of theory we may not reach a like misery.

Wounded affection there is sure to be, but this could be reduced to a modicum if we could preserve a sense of the relation of the individual to the family, and of the latter to society, and if we had been given a code of ethics dealing with these larger relationships, instead of a code designed to apply so exclusively to relationships obtaining only between individuals.

Doubtless the clashes and jars which we all feel most keenly are those which occur when two standards of morals, both honestly held and believed in, are brought sharply together. The awkwardness and constraint we experience when two standards of conventions and manners clash but feebly prefigure this deeper difference.

Charlotte Perkins Gilman
1860-1935

Source: *Women and Economics* (1898)
Selection: "Chapter VI"

Introduction: *Charlotte Perkins Gilman was a prominent American sociologist, feminist, social activist, lecturer, and writer of nonfiction, novels, short stories, and poetry. Born in Hartford, CT, she had a difficult childhood because her father, Frederick Beecher Perkins—a relative of the famous writer Harriet Beecher Stowe—abandoned the family and left Charlotte's mother alone to raise two children on her own.*

In 1884, at the age of 24, Gilman married an artist, Charles Stetson, and they had a daughter, Katherine. Subsequently, Gilman experienced severe depression for which she had unusual treatments that presumably inspired her best-known short story, "The Yellow Wall-Paper" (1892). Six years after her first marriage, Gilman wed for the second time, to her cousin George Gilman, and the marriage lasted until his death in 1934. The next year, upon discovering she had inoperable breast cancer, Gilman committed suicide, in Pasadena, CA.

In her roles as a feminist and activist, Gilman urged women to gain economic independence; and as a social theorist she wrote about the relationship between women and the economic system in several books, including Women and Economics *(1898), which is generally considered her greatest sociological work;* The Home: Its Work and Influence *(1903); and* Does a Man Support His Wife? *(1915). Along with writing books, Gilman established* The Forerunner, *a magazine published from 1909 to 1916 that featured essays, opinion pieces, fiction, poetry and excerpts from novels, and allowed her to express her ideas on women's issues and social reform.*

In her sociological analyses, Gilman mainly focused on gender stratification and inequality. She insisted that the "gendered division of labor" in society resulted from the economic system. It produced a "sexuo-economic arrangement," as she called it—an arrangement composed of a ruling class of men and a subordinate class of women. She agreed with Karl Marx that meaningful work is essential for human self-realization, but she differed from Marx in being concerned with how women—not the working class—were alienated from the human species. She attributed such alienation to women being kept isolated in private households and compelled to perform nonproductive work. This view is expressed in the reading below from Women and Economics, *which includes a theory ensconced in an evolutionary viewpoint. The reading also shows why Gilman insisted that the sexuo-economic arrangement of her time was wasteful in terms of productivity and efficiency, and resulted in the physical and emotional exploitation of women. To solve this problem, Gilman said that women had to become economically emancipated—especially through opportunities to work for wages outside the household—and for the traditional household to be restructured in a responsible and rational way by professionalizing tasks such as child care and cooking.*

*

Society is confronted in this age with most pressing problems in economics, and we need the fullest understanding of the factors involved. These problems are almost wholly social rather than physical, and concern not the capacity of a given society to produce and distribute enough wealth for its maintenance, but some maladjustment of internal processes which checks that production and distribution, and developes such irregular and morbid processes of innutrition, malnutrition, and over-nutrition as continually to injure the health and activity of the social organism. Our difficulty about wealth is not in getting it out of the earth, but in getting it away from one another. We have phenomena before us in the development of social economic relations analogous to those accompanying our development in sex-relation.

In the original constituents of society, the human animal in its primitive state, economic processes were purely individual. The amount of food obtained by a given man bore direct relation to his own personal exertions. Other men were to him merely undesirable competitors for the same goods; and the fewer these competitors were, the more goods remained for him. Therefore, he killed as many of his rivals as possible. Given a certain supply of needed food, as the edible beasts or fruits in a forest, and a certain number of individuals to get this food, each by his own exertions, it follows that, the more numerous the individuals, the less food to be obtained by each; and, conversely, the fewer the individuals, the more food to be obtained by each. . . . That time is forever past. The basic condition of human life is union: the organic social relation, the interchange of functional service, wherein the individual is most advantaged, not by his own exertions for his own goods, but by the exchange of his exertions with the exertions of others for goods produced by them together. We are not treating here of any communistic theory as to the equitable division of the wealth produced, but of a clear truth in social economics—that wealth is a social product. Whatever one may believe as to what should be done with the wealth of the world, no one can deny that the production of this wealth requires the combined action of many individuals. From the simplest combination of strength that enables many men to overcome the mammoth or to lift the stone—an achievement impossible to one alone—to the subtle and complex interchange of highly specialized skilled labor which makes possible our modern house, the progress of society rests upon the increasing collectivity of human labor.

The evolution of organic life goes on in geometrical progression: cells combine, and form organs; organs combine, and form organisms; organisms combine, and form organizations. Society is an organization. Society is the fourth power of the cell. It is composed of individual animals of genus homo, living in organic relation. The course of social evolution is the gradual establishment of organic relation between individuals, and this organic relation rests on purely economic grounds. In the simplest combination of primordial cells, the force that drew and held them together was that of economic necessity. It profited them to live in combination. Those that did so survived and those that did not perished. So with the appearance of the most elaborate organisms: it profited them to become a complex bundle of members and organs in indivisible relation. A creature so constructed survived, where the same amount of living matter unorganized would have perished. And so it is, literally and exactly, in a complex society, with all its elaborate specialization of individuals in arts and crafts, trades and professions. A society so constructed survives, where the same number of living beings, unorganized, would perish. The specialization of labor and exchange of product in a social body is identical in its nature with the specialization and exchange of function in an individual body. This process, on orderly lines of evolution, involves the gradual subordination of individual effort for individual good to the collective effort for the collective good—not from any so-called "altruism," but from the economic necessities of the case. It is as natural, as "selfish," for society so to live, the individual citizens working together for the social good, as for one's own body to live by the hands and feet, teeth and eyes, heart and lungs, working together for the individual good. Social evolution tends to an increasing specialization in structure and function, and to an increasing inter-dependence of the component parts, with a correlative decrease through disuse of the once valuable process of individual struggle for success; and this is based absolutely on the advantage to the individual as well as to the social body.

But, as we study this process of development, noting with admiration the progressive changes in human relation, the new functions, the extended structure, the increase of sensation in the socialized individuals with its enormous possibilities of joy and healthful sensitiveness to pain, we are struck by the visible presence of some counter-force, acting against the normal development and producing most disadvantageous effects. As in our orderly progress in social sex-development we are checked by the tenacious hold of rudimentary impulses artificially maintained by false conditions, so in our orderly progress in social economic development we see the same peculiar survival of rudimentary impulses, which should have been long since easily outgrown. It is no longer of advantage to the individual to struggle for his own gain at the expense of others: his gain now requires the co-ordinate efforts of these others; yet he continues so to struggle.

In this lack of adjustment between the individual and the social interest lies our economic trouble. . . . This failure to recognize or, at least, to act up to a recognition of social interests, owing to the disproportionate pressure of individual interests, is the underlying cause of our economic distress. As society is composed of individuals, we must look to them for the action causing these morbid social processes; and, as individuals act under the pressure of conditions, we must look to the conditions affecting the individuals for the causes of their action.

In general, under social law, men develope right action; but some hidden spring seems to force them continually into wrong action. We have our hand upon this hidden spring in the sexuo-economic relation. If we had remained on an individual economic basis, the evil influence would have had far less ill effect; but, as we grow into the social economic relation, it increases with our civilization. The sex-relation is primarily and finally individual. It is a physical relation between individual bodies; and, while it may also extend to a psychical relation between individual souls, it does not become a social relation, though it does change its personal development to suit social needs.

In all its processes, to all its results, the sex-relation is personal, working through individuals upon individuals, and developing individual traits and characteristics, to the great advantage of society. The qualities developed by social relation are built into the race through the sex-relation, but the sex-relation itself is wholly personal. Our economic relation, on the contrary, though originally individual, becomes through social evolution increasingly collective. By combining the human sex-relation with the human economic relation, we have combined a permanently individual process with a progressively collective one. This involves a strain on both, which increases in direct proportion to our socialization, and, so far, has resulted in the ultimate destruction of the social organism acted upon by such irreconcilable forces.

As has been shown, this combination has affected the sex-relation of individuals by bringing into it a tendency to collectivism with economic advantage, best exhibited in our distinctive racial phenomenon of prostitution. On the other hand, it has affected the economic relation of society by bringing into it a tendency to individualism with sex-advantage, best exhibited in the frequent practice of sacrificing public good to personal gain, that the individual may thereby "support his family." We are so used to considering it the first duty of a man to support his family that it takes a very glaring instance of bribery and corruption in their interests to shake our conviction; but, as a sociological law, every phase of the prostitution of public service to private gain, from the degradation of the artist to the exploitation of the helpless unskilled laborer, marks a diseased social action. Our social status rests upon our common consent, common action, common submission to the common will. No individual interests can stand for a moment against the interests of the common weal, either when war demands the last sacrifice of individual property and life or when peace requires the absolute submission of individual property and life to common law—the fixed expression of the people's will. The maintenance of "law and order" involves the very spirit of socialism—the sinking of personal interest in common interest. All this rests upon the evolution of the social spirit, the keen sense of social duty, the conscientious fulfillment of social service; and it is here that the excessive individualism maintained by our sexuo-economic relation enters as a strong and increasingly disadvantageous social factor. We have dimly recognized the irreconcilability of the sex-relation with economic relations on both sides—in our sharp condemnation of making the sex-functions openly commercial, and in the drift toward celibacy in collective institutions. Bodies of men or women, actuated by the highest religious impulses, desiring to live nobly and to serve society, have always recognized something antagonistic in the sex-relation. They have thought it inherent in the relation itself, not seeing that it was the economic side which made it reactionary. Yet this action practically admitted by the continued existent of communal societies where the sex-relation did exist, in an unacknowledged form, and without the element of economic exchange. It is admitted also by the noble and self-sacrificing devotion of married missionaries of the Protestant Church, who are supported by contributions. If the missionary were obliged to earn his wife's living and his own, he could do little mission work.

The highest human attributes are perfectly compatible with the sex-relation, but not with the sexuo-economic relation. We see this opposition again in the tendency to collectivity in bodies of single men—their comradeship, equality, and mutual helpfulness as compared with the attitude of the same men toward one another, when married. This is why the quality of "organizability" is stronger in men than in women; their common economic interests force them into relation, while the isolated and even antagonistic economic interests of women keep them from it. . . .

On the woman's side we are steadily maintaining the force of primitive individual competition in the world as against the tendency of social progress to develope co-operation in its place, and this tendency of course is inherited by their sons. On the man's side the same effect is produced through another feature of the relation. The tendency to individualism with sex-advantage is developed in man by an opposite process to that operating on the woman. She gets her living by getting a husband. He gets his wife by getting a living. It is to her individual economic advantage to secure a mate. It is to his individual sex-advantage to secure economic gain. The sex-functions to her have become economic functions. Economic functions to him have become sex-

100

functions. This has confounded our natural economic competition, inevitably growing into economic co-operation, with the element of sex-competition—an entirely different force.

Competition among males, with selection by the female of the superior male, is the process of sexual selection, and works to racial improvement. So far as the human male competes freely with his peers in higher and higher activities, and the female chooses the winner, so far we are directly benefited. But there is a radical distinction between sex-competition and marriage by purchase. In the first the male succeeds by virtue of what he can do; in the second, by virtue of what he can get. The increased power to do, transmitted to the young, is of racial advantage. But mere possessions, with no question as to the method of their acquisition, are not necessarily of advantage to the individual as a father. To make the sexual gain of the male rest on his purchasing power puts the immense force of sex-competition into the field of social economics, not only as an incentive to labor and achievement, which is good, but as an incentive to individual gain, however obtained, which is bad; thus accounting for our multiplied and intensified desire to get—the inordinate greed of our industrial world. . . .

The foregoing distinction should be clearly held in mind. Legitimate sex-competition brings out all that is best in man. To please her, to win her, he strives to do his best. But the economic dependence of the female upon the male, with its ensuing purchasability, does not so affect a man: it puts upon him the necessity for getting things, not for doing them. In the lowest grades of labor, where there is no getting without doing and where the laborer always does more than he gets, this works less palpable evil than in the higher grades, the professions and arts, where the most valuable work is always ahead of the market, and where to work for the market involves a lowering of standards. The young artist or poet or scientific student works for his work's sake, for art, for science, and so for the best good of society. But the artist or student married must get gain, must work for those who will pay; and those who will pay are not those who lift and bear forward the standard of progress. Community of interest is quite possible with those who are working most disinterestedly for the social good; but bring in the sex-relation, and all such solidarity disintegrates—resolves itself into the tiny groups of individuals united on a basis of sex-union, and briskly acting in their own immediate interests at anybody's or everybody's expense.

The social perception of the evil resultant from the intrusion of sex-influence upon racial action has found voice in the heartless proverb, "There is no evil without a woman at the bottom of it." When a man's work goes wrong, his hopes fail, his ambitions sink, cynical friends inquire, "Who is she?" It is not for nothing that a man's best friends sigh when he marries, especially if he is a man of genius. This judgment of the world has obtained side by side with its equal faith in the ennobling influence of woman. The world is quite right. It does not have to be consistent. Both judgments are correct. Woman affecting society through the sex-relation or through her individual economic relation is an ennobling influence. Woman affecting society through our perverse combination of the two becomes a strange influence, indeed.

One of the amusing minor results of these conditions is that, while we have observed the effect of marriage upon social economic relation and the effect of social economic relation upon marriage—seeing that the devoted servant of the family was a poor servant of society and that the devoted servant of society was a poor servant of the family, seeing the successful collectivity of celibate institutions—we have jumped to the conclusion that collective prosperity was conditioned upon celibacy, and that we did not want it. That is why the popular mind is so ready to associate socialistic theories with injury to marriage. Having seen that marriage makes us less collective, we infer conversely that collectivity will make us less married—that it will "break up the home," "strike at the roots of the family."

When we make plain to ourselves that a pure, lasting, monogamous sex-union can exist without bribe or purchase, without the manacles of economic dependence, and that men and women so united in sex-relation will still be free to combine with others in economic relation, we shall not regard devotion to humanity as an unnatural sacrifice, nor collective prosperity as a thing to fear.

Besides this maintenance of primeval individualism in the growing collectivity of social economic process and the introduction of the element of sex-combat into the narrowing field of industrial competition, there is another side to the evil influence of the sexuo-economic relation upon social development. This is in the attitude of woman as a non-productive consumer.

In the industrial evolution of the human race, that marvellous and subtle drawing out and interlocking of special functions which constitute the organic life of society, we find that production and consumption go hand in hand; and production comes first. One cannot consume what has not been produced. Economic production is the natural expression of human energy—not sex-energy at all, but race-energy—the unconscious functioning of the social organism. Socially organized human beings tend to produce, as a gland to secrete: it is the essential nature of the relation. The creative impulse, the desire to make, to express the inner thought in outer form, "just for the work's sake, no use at all in the work!" this is the distinguishing character of humanity. "I want to mark!" cries the child, demanding the pencil. He does not want to eat. He wants to mark. He is not seeking to get something into himself, but to put something out of himself. He generally wants to do whatever he sees done—to make pie-crust or to make shavings, as it happens. The pie he may eat, the shavings not; but he likes to make both. This is the natural process of production, and is followed by the natural process of consumption, where practicable. But consumption is not the main end, the governing force. Under this organic social law, working naturally, we have the evolution of those arts and crafts in the exercise of which consists our human living, and on the product of which we live. So does society evolve within itself—secrete as it were—the social structure with all its complex machinery; and we function therein as naturally as so many glands, other things being equal.

But other things are not equal. Half the human race is denied free productive expression, is forced to confine its productive human energies to the same channels as its reproductive sex-energies. Its creative skill is confined to the level of immediate personal bodily service, to the making of clothes and preparing of food for individuals. No social service is possible. While its power of production is checked, its power of consumption is inordinately increased by the showering upon it of the "unearned increment" of masculine gifts. For the woman there is, first, no free production allowed; and, second, no relation maintained between what she does produce and what she consumes. She is forbidden to make, but encouraged to take. Her industry is not the natural output of creative energy, not the work she does because she has the inner power and strength to do it; nor is her industry even the measure of her gain. She has, of course, the natural desire to consume; and to that is set no bar save the capacity or the will of her husband.

Thus we have painfully and laboriously evolved and carefully maintain among us an enormous class of non-productive consumers—a class which is half the world, and mother of the other half. We have built into the constitution of the human race the habit and desire of taking, as divorced from its natural precursor and concomitant of making. We have made for ourselves this endless array of "horse-leech's daughters, crying, Give! give!" To consume food, to consume clothes, to consume houses and furniture and decorations and ornaments and amusements, to take and take and take forever, from one man if they are virtuous, from many if they are vicious, but always to take and never to think of giving anything in return except their womanhood—this is the enforced condition of the mothers of the race. What wonder that their sons go into business "for what there is in it"! What wonder that the world is full of the desire to get as much as possible and to give as little as possible! What wonder, either, that the glory and sweetness of love are but a name among us, with here and there a strange and beautiful exception, of which our admiration proves the rarity!

Between the brutal ferocity of excessive male energy struggling in the marketplace as in a battlefield and the unnatural greed generated by the perverted condition of female energy, it is not remarkable that the industrial evolution of humanity has shown peculiar symptoms. One of the minor effects of this last condition—this limiting of female industry to close personal necessities, and this tendency of her over-developed sex-nature to overestimate the so-called "duties of her position"—has been to produce an elaborate devotion to individuals and their personal needs—not to the understanding and developing of their higher natures, but to the intensification of their bodily tastes and pleasure. The wife and mother, pouring the rising tide of racial power into the same old channels that were allowed her primitive ancestors, constantly ministers to the physical needs of her family with a ceaseless and concentrated intensity. They like it, of course. But it maintains in the individuals of the race an exaggerated sense of the importance of food and clothes and ornaments to themselves, without at all including a knowledge of their right use and value to us all. It developes personal selfishness.

Again, the consuming female, debarred from any free production, unable to estimate the labor involved in the making of what she so lightly destroys, and her consumption limited mainly to those things which minister to physical pleasure, creates a market for sensuous decoration and personal ornament, for all that is luxurious and enervating, and for a false and capricious variety in such supplies, which operates as a most deadly check to true industry and true art. As the priestess of the temple of consumption, as the limitless demander of things to use up, her economic influence is reactionary and injurious. Much, very much, of the current of useless production in which our economic energies run waste—man's strength poured out like water on the sand—depends on the creation and careful maintenance of this false market, this sink into which human labor vanishes with no return. Woman, in her false economic position, reacts injuriously upon industry, upon art, upon science, discovery, and progress. The sexuo-economic relation in its effect on the constitution of the individual keeps alive in us the instincts of savage individualism which we should otherwise have well outgrown. It sexualizes our industrial relation and commercializes our sex-relation. And, in the external effect upon the market, the over-sexed woman, in her unintelligent and ceaseless demands, hinders and perverts the economic development of the world.

Robert Ezra Park
1864-1944

Source: *The City* (1915)
Selection: "The City Plan and Local Organization" and
"Temperament and the Urban Environment"

Introduction: *Robert Ezra Park was a pioneering American sociologist best known for developing the nascent field of sociology at the University of Chicago; his books and articles on the city and "human ecology"—a phrase he coined; and his work with Booker T. Washington. He was born in Harveyville, PA, and raised in Red Wing, MN, before attending the University of Michigan, where he studied philosophy under John Dewey and graduated Phi Beta Kappa, in 1887. In 1889, Park entered Harvard University to study psychology and philosophy, and a year later earned an M.A. in philosophy. He then traveled to Germany where he studied at the University of Berlin and the University of Strasbourg, followed by a few years at the University of Heidelberg, from which he earned his doctoral degree.*

During much of this time, Park had also worked as a muckraking journalist in New York, Denver, and various parts of the Midwest, pursuing his interest in social reform, especially as it pertained to Africans and African-Americans. This interest led him to collaborate with the founder of the Tuskegee Institute, Booker T. Washington, and helped him to establish the National Urban League. In 1901, Park traveled with Washington through Europe, where they studied the dire situation of the European working class and farmers.

In 1914, Park left Tuskegee to join the faculty of the University of Chicago in the Department of Sociology and Anthropology. He remained there about two decades and eventually served as the head of the department. In 1925, became the fifteenth president of what is now known as the American Sociological Association.

Under Park's leadership at Chicago, the school of sociology grew to prominence, including Ernest Burgess and Louis Wirth who, together with Park, created innovative theoretical bases by which to systematically study society.

Robert Ezra Park

Chicago was a perfect environment for Park to study the processes of urbanization, because it was a teeming metropolis with immigrant groups from many nations and cultures that was undergoing rapid industrialization. His studies and theories are recognized as groundbreaking contributions to the developing field of sociology, especially his work on urban life and "human ecology." The latter included analyses of concepts drawn from the science of natural ecology—such as symbiosis, invasion, succession, dominance, superordination, and subordination—which he applied to social life. Park also delineated system-wide social behaviors and dynamics, and was instrumental in drawing sociology away from a normative analysis of society toward a more objective methodology.

Among Park's more notable books are Introduction to the Science of Sociology *(1921), coauthored with Ernest W. Burgess, and* The Immigrant Press and Its Control *(1922). He also wrote many articles, including "The City," which contains the excerpt below. As may be seen, in this article Park not only provides a seminal analysis of urban life but also raises many questions for sociologists who are concerned about urban life to consider.*

*

The City Plan and Local Organization: The city, particularly the modern American city, strikes one at first blush as so little a product of the artless processes of nature and growth that it is difficult to recognize its institutional character. The ground plan of most American cities, for example, is a checker-board. The unit of distance is the block. This geometrical form suggests that the city is a purely artificial construction, which might conceivably be taken apart and put together again, like a house of blocks.

The fact is, however, that the city is rooted in the habits and customs of the people who inhabit it. The consequence is that the city possesses a moral as well as a physical organization, and these two mutually interact in characteristic ways to mold and modify one another. It is the structure of the city which impresses us by its visible vastness and complexity, but this structure has its basis, nevertheless, in human nature, of which it is an expression. On the other hand, this vast organization which has arisen in response to the needs of its inhabitants, once formed, impresses itself upon them as a crude external fact, and forms them, in turn, in accordance with the design and interests which it incorporates.

Robert Ezra Park

The city plan.—It is because the city has what has here been described as its institutional character that there is a limit to the arbitrary modifications which it is possible to make in its physical structure and its moral order.

The city plan, for example, establishes metes and bounds, fixes in a general way the location and character of the city's constructions, and imposes an orderly arrangement, within the city area, upon the buildings which are erected by private initiative as well as by public authority. Within the limitations prescribed, however, the inevitable processes of human nature proceed to give these regions and these buildings a character which it is less easy to control. Under our system of individual ownership, for instance, it is not possible to determine in advance the extent of concentration of population in any given area. The city cannot fix land values, and we leave to private enterprise, for the most part, the task of determining the city's limits and the location of its residential and industrial districts. Personal tastes and convenience, vocational and economic interests, infallibly tend to segregate and thus to classify the populations of great cities. In this way the city acquires an organization which is neither designed nor controlled.

Physical geography, natural advantages, and the means of transportation determine in advance the general outlines of the urban plan. As the city increases in population, the subtler influences of sympathy, rivalry, and economic necessity tend to control the distribution of population. Business and manufacturing seek advantageous locations and draw around them a certain portion of the population. There spring up fashionable residence quarters from which the poorer classes are excluded because of the increased value of the land. Then there grow up slums which are inhabited by great numbers of the poorer classes who are unable to defend themselves from association with the derelict and vicious. In the course of time every section and quarter of the city takes on something of the character and qualities of its inhabitants. Each separate part of the city is inevitably stained with the peculiar sentiments of its population. The effect of this is to convert what was at first a mere geographical expression into a neighborhood, that is to say, a locality with sentiments, traditions, and a history of its own. Within this neighborhood the continuity of the historical processes is somehow maintained. The past imposes itself upon the present and the life of every locality moves on with a certain momentum of its own, more or less independent of the larger circle of life and interests about it.

The organization of the city, the character of the urban environment and of the discipline which it imposes, is finally determined by the size of the population, its concentration and distribution within the city area. For this reason it is important to study the populations of cities, to compare the idiosyncrasies in the development of city populations. Some of the first things we want to know about the city, therefore, are: sources of population; immigration and natural growth; distribution of population within the city as affected by (a) economic, i.e., land, values, (b) sentimental interests, race, vocation, etc.; (c) comparative growths of the population within different portions of the city area, as affected by birth- and death-rates, marriage and divorce, etc.

The neighborhood.—Proximity and neighborly contact are the basis for the simplest and most elementary form of association with which we have to do in the organization of city life. Local interests and associations breed local sentiment, and, under a system which makes residence the basis for participation in the government, the neighborhood becomes the basis of political control. In the social and political organization of the city it is the smallest local unit.

"It is surely one of the most remarkable of all social facts that, coming down from untold ages, there should be this instinctive understanding that the man who establishes his home beside yours begins to have a claim upon your sense of comradeship. The neighborhood is a social unit which, by its clear definition of outline, its inner organic completeness, its hair-trigger reactions, may be fairly considered as functioning like a social mind. The local boss, however autocratic he may be in the larger sphere of the city with the power he gets from the neighborhood, must always be in and of the people; and he is very careful not to try to deceive the local people so far as their local interests are concerned. It is hard to fool a neighborhood about its own affairs."[1]

The neighborhood exists without formal organization. The local improvement society is the structure erected on the basis of the spontaneous neighborhood organization and exists for the purpose of giving expression to the local sentiment.

Under the complex influences of the city life, what may be called the normal neighborhood sentiment has undergone many curious and

interesting changes, and produced many unusual types of local communities. More than that, there are nascent neighborhoods and neighborhoods in process of dissolution. Consider, for example, Fifth Avenue,
New York, which probably never had an improvement association, and
compare with it with 135th Street in the Bronx (where the negro
population is probably more concentrated than in any other single spot in
the world), which is rapidly becoming a very intimate and highly organized community.

It is important to know what are the forces which tend to break up
the tensions, interests, and sentiments which give neighborhoods their
individual character. In general these may be said to be anything and
everything that tends to render the population unstable, to divide and
concentrate attentions upon widely separated objects of interest.

What part of the population is floating?

Of what elements, i.e., races, classes, etc., is this population
composed?

How many people live in hotels, apartments, and tenements?

How many people own their own homes?

What proportion of the population consists of nomads, hobos,
gypsies?

On the other hand, certain urban neighborhoods suffer from
isolation. Efforts have been made at different times to reconstruct and
quicken the life of city neighborhoods and to bring it in touch with the
larger interests of the community. Such is in part the purpose of the
social settlements. These organizations and others which are attempting
to reconstruct city life have developed certain methods and a technique
for stimulating and controlling local communities. We should study, in
connection with the investigation of these agencies, these methods and
this technique, since it is just the method by which objects are practically
controlled that reveals their essential nature, that is to say, their
predictable character. . . .

In many of the European cities, and to some extent in this country,
reconstruction of city life has gone to the length of building garden suburbs, or replacing unhealthful and run-down tenements with model
buildings owned and controlled by the municipality.

In American cities the attempt has been made to renovate evil neighborhoods by the construction of playgrounds and the introduction of supervised sports of various kinds, including municipal dances in municipal dance halls. These and other devices which are intended primarily to elevate the moral tone of the segregated populations of great cities should be studied in connection with the investigation of the neighborhood in general. They should be studied, in short, not merely for their own sake but for what they can reveal to us of human behavior and human nature generally.

Colonies and segregated areas.—In the city environment the neighborhood tends to lose much of the significance which it possessed in simpler and more primitive forms of society. The easy means of communication and of transportation, which enables individuals to distribute their attention and to live at the same time in several different worlds, tends to destroy the permanency and intimacy of the neighborhood. Further than that, where individuals of the same race or of the same vocation live together in segregated groups, neighborhood sentiment tends to fuse together with racial antagonisms and class interests.

In this way physical and sentimental distances reinforce each other, and the influences of local distribution of the population participate with the influences of class and race in the evolution of the social organization. Every great city has its racial colonies, like the Chinatowns of San Francisco and New York, the Little Sicily of Chicago, and various other less pronounced types. In addition to these, most cities have their segregated vice districts, like that which until recently existed in Chicago, and their rendezvous for criminals of various sorts. Every large city has its occupational suburbs like the Stockyards in Chicago, and its residence suburbs like Brookline in Boston, each of which has the size and the character of a complete separate town, village, or city, except that its population is a selected one. Undoubtedly the most remarkable of these cities within cities, of which the most interesting characteristic is that they are composed of persons of the same race, or of persons of different races but of the same social class, is East London, with a population of 2,000,000 laborers. . . .

In the older cities of Europe, where the processes of segregation have gone farther, neighborhood distinctions are likely to be more marked than they are in America. East London is a city of a single class, but within the limits of that city the population is segregated again and again by racial and vocational interests. Neighborhood sentiment, deeply rooted in local tradition and in local custom, exercises a decisive selective influence upon city population and shows itself ultimately in a marked way in the characteristics of the inhabitants.

What we want to know of these neighborhoods, racial communities, and segregated city areas, existing within or on the outer edge of great cities, is what we want to know of all other social groups.

What are the elements of which they are composed?

To what extent are they the product of a selective process?

How do people get in and out of the group thus formed?

What are the relative permanence and stability of their populations?

What about the age, sex, and social condition of the people?

What about the children? How many of them are born, and how many of them remain?

What is the history of the neighborhood? What is there in the sub-consciousness—in the forgotten or dimly remembered experiences—of this neighborhood which determines its sentiments and attitudes?

What is there in clear consciousness, i.e., what are its avowed sentiments, doctrines, etc.?

What does it regard as matter of fact? What is news? What is the general run of attention? What models does it imitate and are these within or without the group?

What is the social ritual, i.e., what things must one do in the neighborhood in order to escape being regarded with suspicion or looked upon as peculiar?

Who are the leaders? What interests of the neighborhood do they incorporate in themselves and what is the technique by which they exercise control? . . .

Temperament and the Urban Environment: Great cities have always been the melting-pots of races and of cultures. Out of the vivid and subtle interactions of which they have been the centers, there have come the newer breeds and the newer social types. The great cities of the United States, for example, have drawn from the isolation of their native villages great masses of the rural populations of Europe and America. Under the shock of the new contacts the latent energies of these primitive peoples have been released, and the subtler processes of interaction have brought into existence not merely vocational but temperamental types.

Mobilization of the individual man.—Transportation and communication have effected, among many other silent but far-reaching changes, what I have called the "mobilization of the individual man." They have multiplied the opportunities of the individual man for contact and for association with his fellows, but they have made these contacts and associations more transitory and less stable. A very large part of the populations of great cities, including those who make their homes in tenements and apartment houses, live much as people do in some great hotel, meeting but not knowing one another. The effect of this is to substitute fortuitous and casual relationship for the more intimate and permanent associations of the smaller community.

Under these circumstances the individual's status is determined to a considerable degree by conventional signs—by fashion and "front"—and the art of life is largely reduced to skating on thin surfaces and a scrupulous study of style and manners.

Not only transportation and communication, but the segregation of the urban population tends to facilitate the mobility of the individual man. The processes of segregation establish moral distances which make the city a mosaic of little worlds which touch but do not interpenetrate. This makes it possible for individuals to pass quickly and easily from one moral milieu to another and encourages the fascinating but dangerous experiment of living at the same time in several different contiguous, perhaps, but widely separated worlds. All this tends to give to city life a superficial and adventitious character; it tends to complicate social relationships and to produce new and divergent individual types. It introduces, at the same time, an element of chance and adventure, which adds to the stimulus of city life and gives it for young and fresh nerves a peculiar attractiveness. The lure of great cities is perhaps a consequence of stimulations which act directly upon the reflexes. As a type of human behavior it may be explained, like the attraction of the flame for the moth, as a sort of tropism.

The attraction of the metropolis is due in part, however, to the fact that in the long run every individual finds somewhere among the varied manifestations of city life the sort of environment in which he expands and feels at ease; finds, in short, the moral climate in which his peculiar nature obtains the stimulations that bring his innate qualities to full and free expression. It is, I suspect, motives of this kind which have their basis, not in interest nor even in sentiment, but in something more fundamental and primitive which draw many, if not most, of the young men and young women from the security of their homes in the country into the big, booming confusion and excitement of city life. In a small community it is the normal man, the man without eccentricity or genius, who seems most likely to succeed. The small community often tolerates eccentricity. The city, on the contrary, rewards it. Neither the criminal, the defective, nor the genius has the same opportunity to develop his innate disposition in a small town that he invariably finds in a great city.

Fifty years ago every village had one or two eccentric characters who were treated ordinarily with a benevolent toleration, but who were regarded meanwhile as impracticable and queer. These exceptional individuals lived an isolated existence, cut off by their very eccentricities, whether of genius or of defect, from genuinely intimate intercourse with their fellows. If they had the making of criminals, the restraints and inhibitions of the small community rendered them harmless. If they had the stuff of genius in them, they remained sterile for lack of appreciation or opportunity. . . .

In the city many of these divergent types now find a milieu in which for good or for ill their dispositions and talents parturate and bear fruit.

In the investigation of those exceptional and temperamental types which the city has produced, we should seek to distinguish, as far as possible, between those abstract mental qualities upon which technical excellence is based and those more fundamental native characteristics which find expression in temperament. We may therefore ask:

To what extent are the moral qualities of individuals based on native character? To what extent are they conventionalized habits imposed upon by them or taken over by them from the group?

What are the native qualities and characteristics upon which the moral or immoral character accepted and conventionalized by the group are based?

What connection or what divorce appears to exist between mental and moral qualities in the groups and in the individuals composing them?

Are criminals as a rule of a lower order of intelligence than non-criminals? If so, what types of intelligence are associated with different types of crime? For example, do professional burglars and professional confidence men represent different mental types?

What are the effects upon these different types of isolation and of mobility, of stimulus and of repression?

To what extent can playgrounds and other forms of recreation supply the stimulation which is otherwise sought for in vicious pleasures?

To what extent can vocational guidance assist individuals in finding vocations in which they will be able to obtain a free expression of their temperamental qualities?

The moral region.—It is inevitable that individuals who seek the same forms of excitement, whether that excitement be furnished by a horse race or by grand opera, should find themselves from time to time in the same places. The result of this is that, in the organization which city life spontaneously assumes, a disposition of the population manifests itself to segregate itself, not merely in accordance with its interests but in accordance with its tastes or its temperaments. The resulting distribution of the population is likely to be quite different from that brought about by occupational interests or economic conditions.

Every neighborhood, under the influences which tend to distribute and segregate city populations, may assume the character of a "moral region." Such, for example, are the vice districts, which are found in most cities. A moral region is not necessarily a place of abode. It may be a mere rendezvous, a place of resort.

In order to understand the forces which in every large city tend to develop these detached milieus, in which vagrant and suppressed impulses, passions, and ideals emancipate themselves from the dominant moral order, it is necessary to refer to the fact or theory of latent impulses of men.

The fact seems to be that men are brought into the world with all the passions, instincts, and appetites uncontrolled and undisciplined. Civilization, in the interests of the common welfare, demands the suppression sometimes, and the control always, of these wild, natural dispositions. In the process of imposing its discipline upon the individual, in making over the individual in accordance with the accepted community model, much is suppressed altogether, and much more finds a vicarious expression in forms that are socially valuable, or at least innocuous. It is at this point that sport, play, and art function. They permit the individual to purge himself by means of symbolic expression of these wild and suppressed impulses. This is the catharsis of which Aristotle wrote in his *Poetic* and which has been given new and more positive significance by the investigations of Sigmund Freud and the Psycho-Analysts.[2]

No doubt many other social phenomena, such as strikes, wars, popular elections, and religious revivals, perform a similar function in releasing the subconscious tensions. But within smaller communities where social relations are more intimate and inhibitions more imperative, there are many exceptional individuals who find within the limits of the communal activity no normal and healthful expression of their individual aptitudes and temperaments.

The causes which give rise to what are here described as "moral regions" are due in part to the restrictions which urban life imposes; in part to the license which these same conditions offer. We have until very recently given much consideration to the temptations of city life, but we have not given the same consideration to the effects of inhibitions and suppressions of natural impulses and instincts under the changed conditions of metropolitan life. For one thing, children which in the country are counted as an asset become in the city a liability. Aside from this fact it is very much more difficult to rear a family in the city than on the farm. Marriage takes place later in the city, and sometimes it doesn't take place at all. These facts have consequences the significance of which we are as yet wholly unable to estimate.

Investigation of the problems involved might well begin by a study and comparison of the characteristic types of social organization which exist in the regions referred to.

What are the external facts in regard to the life in Bohemia, the Half-World, the Red-Light District, and other "moral regions," less pronounced in character?

What is the nature of the vocations which connect themselves with the ordinary life of these regions?

What are the characteristic mental types which are attracted by the freedom which they offer?

How do individuals find their way into these regions? How do they escape from them?

To what extent are the regions referred to the product of the license; to what extent are they due to the restrictions imposed by city life on the natural man?

Temperament and social contagion.—What lends special importance to the segregation of the poor, the vicious, the criminal, and exceptional persons generally, which is so characteristic a feature of city life, is the fact that social contagion tends to stimulate in divergent types the common temperamental differences, and to suppress characters which unite them with the normal types about them. Association with others of their own ilk provides also not merely a stimulus, but a moral support for the traits they have in common which they would not find in a less select society. . . .

We must then accept these "moral regions" and the more or less eccentric and exceptional people who inhabit them, in a sense, at least, as part of the natural if not the normal life of a city.

It is not necessary to understand by the expression "moral region" a place or a society that is either necessarily criminal or abnormal. It is intended rather to apply to regions in which a divergent moral code prevails, because it is a region in which the people who inhabit it are dominated, as people are ordinarily not dominated, by a taste or by a passion or by some interest which has its roots directly in the original nature of the individual. It may be an art, like music, or a sport, like horse racing. Such a region would differ from other social groups by the fact that its interests are more immediate and more fundamental. For this reason its differences are likely to be due to moral rather than intellectual isolation.

Because of the opportunity it offers, particularly to the exceptional and abnormal types of man, a great city tends to spread out and lay bare to the public view in a massive manner all the characters and traits which are ordinarily obscured and suppressed in smaller communities. The city, in short, shows the good and evil in human nature in excess. It is this fact, perhaps, more than any other which justifies the view that would make of the city a laboratory or clinic in which human nature and social processes may be most conveniently and profitably studied.

[1] Robert A. Woods, "The Neighborhood in Social Reconstruction," Papers and Proceedings of the Eighth Annual Meeting of the American Sociological Society, 1913.

[2] Cf. Dr. Sigmund Freud, *The Interpretation of Dreams*.

Franz Oppenheimer
1863-1931

Source: *The State* (1914)
Selection: "The State"

Introduction: *Franz Oppenheimer was born to a rabbi in a suburb of Berlin, but he chose medicine as his first career, not religion, and received the M.D. degree in 1885. Soon afterwards, however, he developed an interest in political and economic affairs, which came to dominate his professional life. In 1902 he met Theodor Herzl, considered to be the father of political Zionism, who invited Oppenheimer to talk at the Sixth Zionist Congress in 1903 about the application of his ideas to land settlement in Palestine. This ultimately resulted in Oppenheimer being one of the theoretical founders of the kibbutz system. His passion for political, economic, and sociological matters led him to earn the Ph.D. in 1908 at the University of Kiel, with a thesis about the economist David Ricardo, and a year later he became a lecturer at the University of Berlin.*

After World War I began, Oppenheimer became chairman of a committee established by a group of German Zionists, whose purpose it was to safeguard the Jews in Russian territory occupied by the German force. By 1919 he was appointed full professor of economics and sociology at the University of Frankfurt. A decade later he retired due to ill health and moved to a rural settlement near Berlin. In 1933 he left Germany, along with many of his academic colleagues, and found employment as a visiting professor in France, Palestine, and the United States. He died in Los Angeles.

Oppenheimer viewed sociology as a comparative science whose ultimate goal is to formulate laws to explain societal change, through the analysis of quantitative and qualitative historical and current subject matter about our collective social life. One of the great changes in history, he claimed, was when nomadic tribes of herdsmen and maritime nomads (e.g., Vikings) began to subjugate sedentary populations to the east and west— conquests that led to monopolies, such as land monopolies, tribute payment, and exploitation, and resulted in various forms of the state.

Oppenheimer claimed that throughout history there were various, successive forms of the state, leading to the modern state of his time. As he explained the progression, early in history conquerors and their conquered

were integrated into a larger society that was held together by the "prim-
itive state," in which the process of integration was implemented through
social stratification by class and status. The "primitive state" was followed
by the ancient Mediterranean "seacoast state," which was eventually dis-
placed by agrarian capitalism combined with slavery. These forms of the
state were followed by feudal society, the estate society, early modern
absolutism, and the modern constitutional state, which emerged during the
revolutions in England (1649), France (1789), other European countries
(1848), and Russia (1905). These revolutions led to the end of the legal
division of societies into estates but the land monopoly remained.

Oppenheimer acknowledged his theoretical indebtedness to socio-
logical pioneers such as Saint-Simon, Gumplowicz, and Marx. Although his
own theories are heavily steeped in Marxian analyses, he differed with Marx
in fundamental ways about the origin of the state and class divisions, as may
be seen in the following reading from his most famous work, The State.

*

Theories of the State: The following may be stated as a ruling concept, especially prevalent in university teaching, of the origin and essence of the State. It represents a view which, in spite of manifold attacks, is still affirmed.

It is maintained that the State is an organization of human community life, which originates by reason of a social instinct implanted in men by nature (Stoic Doctrine); or else is brought about by an irresistible impulse to end the "war of all against all," and to coerce the savage, who opposes organized effort, to a peaceable community life in place of the anti-social struggle in which all budding shoots of advancement are destroyed (Epicurean Doctrine). These two apparently irreconcilable concepts were fused by the intermediation of medieval philosophy. This, founded on theologic reasoning and belief in the Bible, developed the opinion that man, originally and by nature a social creature, is, through original sin, the fratricide of Cain and the transgression at the tower of Babel, divided into innumerable tribes, which fight to the hilt, until they unite peaceably as a State.

This view is utterly untenable. It confuses the logical concept of a class with some subordinate species thereof. Granted that the State is one form of organized political cohesion, it is also to be remembered that it is a form having specific characteristics. Every state in history was or is a state of classes, a polity of superior and inferior social groups, based upon distinctions either of rank or of property. This phenomenon must, then, be called the "State." With it alone history occupies itself.

We should, therefore, be justified in designating every other form of political organization by the same term, without further differentiation, had there never existed any other than a class-state, or were it the only conceivable form. At least, proof might properly be called for, to show that each conceivable political organization, even though originally it did not represent a polity of superior and inferior social and economic classes, since it is of necessity subject to inherent laws of development, must in the end be resolved into the specific class form of history. Were such proof forthcoming, it would offer in fact only one form of political amalgamation, calling in turn for differentiation at various stages of development, *viz.*, the preparatory stage, when class distinction does not exist, and the stage of maturity, when it is fully developed.

Former students of the philosophy of the State were dimly aware of this problem. And they tried to adduce the required proof, that because of inherent tendencies of development, every human political organization must gradually become a class-state. Philosophers of the canon law handed this theory down to philosophers of the law of nature. From these, through the mediation of Rousseau, it became a part of the teachings of the economists; and even to this day it rules their views and diverts them from the facts.

This assumed proof is based upon the concept of a "primitive accumulation," or an original store of wealth, in lands and in movable property, brought about by means of purely economic forces; a doctrine justly derided by Karl Marx as a "fairy tale." Its scheme of reasoning approximates this:

Somewhere, in some far-stretching, fertile country, a number of free men, of equal status, form a union for mutual protection. Gradually they differentiate into property classes. Those best endowed with strength, wisdom, capacity for saving, industry and caution, slowly acquire a basic amount of real or movable property; while the stupid and less efficient, and those given to carelessness and waste, remain without possessions. The well-to-do lend their productive property to the less well-off in return for tribute, either ground-rent or profit, and become thereby continually richer, while the others always remain poor. These differences in possession gradually develop social class distinctions; since everywhere the rich have preference, while they alone have the time and the means to devote to public affairs and to turn the laws administered by them to their own advantage. Thus, in time, there develops a ruling and property-owning estate, and a proletariate, a class without property. The primitive state of free and equal fellows becomes a class-state, by an inherent law of development, because in every conceivable mass of men there are, as may readily be seen, strong and weak, clever and foolish, cautious and wasteful ones.

This seems quite plausible, and it coincides with the experience of our daily life. It is not at all unusual to see an especially gifted member of the lower class rise from his former surroundings, and even attain a leading position in the upper class; or conversely, to see some spendthrift or weaker member of the higher group "lose his class" and drop into the proletariate.

And yet this entire theory is utterly mistaken; it is a "fairy tale," or it is a class theory used to justify the privileges of the upper classes. The class-state never originated in this fashion, and never could have so originated. History shows that it did not; and economics shows deductively, with a testimony absolute, mathematical and binding, that it could not. A simple problem in elementary arithmetic shows that the assumption of an original accumulation is totally erroneous, and has nothing to do with the development of the class-state.

The proof is as follows: All teachers of natural law, etc., have unanimously declared that the differentiation into income-receiving classes and propertyless classes can only take place when all fertile lands have been occupied. For so long as man has ample opportunity to take up unoccupied land, "no one," says Turgot, "would think of entering the service of another;" we may add, "at least for wages, which are not apt to be higher than the earnings of an independent peasant working an unmortgaged and sufficiently large property;" while mortgaging is not possible as long as land is yet free for the working or taking, as free as air and water. Matter that is obtainable for the taking has no value that enables it to be pledged, since no one loans on things that can be had for nothing.

Franz Oppenheimer

The philosophers of natural law, then, assumed that complete occupancy of the ground must have occurred quite early, because of the natural increase of an originally small population. They were under the impression that at their time, in the eighteenth century, it had taken place many centuries previous, and they naïvely deduced the existing class aggroupment from the assumed conditions of that long-past point of time. It never entered their heads to work out their problem; and with few exceptions their error has been copied by sociologists, historians and economists. It is only quite recently that my figures were worked out, and they are truly astounding.

We can determine with approximate accuracy the amount of land of average fertility in the temperate zone, and also what amount is sufficient to enable a family of peasants to exist comfortably, or how much such a family can work with its own forces, without engaging outside help or permanent farm servants. At the time of the migration of the barbarians (350 to 750 A.D.), the lot of each able-bodied man was about thirty morgen (equal to twenty acres) on average lands, on very good ground only ten to fifteen morgen (equal to seven or ten acres), four morgen being equal to one hectare. Of this land, at least a third, and sometimes a half, was left uncultivated each year. The remainder of the fifteen to twenty morgen sufficed to feed and fatten into giants the immense families of these child-producing Germans, and this in spite of the primitive technique, whereby at least half the productive capacity of a day was lost. Let us assume that, in these modern times, thirty morgen (equal to twenty acres) for the average peasant suffices to support a family. We have then assumed a block of land sufficiently large to meet any objection. Modern Germany, populated as it is, contains an agricultural area of thirty-four million hectares (equal to eighty-four million, fifteen thousand, four hundred and eighty acres). The agricultural population, including farm laborers and their families, amounts to seventeen million; so that, assuming five persons to a family and an equal division of the farm lands, each family would have ten hectares (equal to twenty-five acres). In other words, not even in the Germany of our own day would the point have been reached where, according to the theories of the adherents of natural law, differentiation into classes would begin.

Apply the same process to countries less densely settled, such, for example, as the Danube States, Turkey, Hungary and Russia, and still

123

more astounding results will appear. As a matter of fact, there are still on the earth's surface seventy-three billion, two hundred million hectares (equal to one hundred eighty billion, eight hundred eighty million and four hundred sixteen thousand acres); dividing into the first amount the number of human beings of all professions whatever, *viz.*, one billion, eight hundred million, every family of five persons could possess about thirty morgen (equal to eighteen and a half acres), and still leave about two-thirds of the planet unoccupied.

If, therefore, purely economic causes are ever to bring about a differentiation into classes by the growth of a propertyless laboring class, the time has not yet arrived; and the critical point at which ownership of land will cause a natural scarcity is thrust into the dim future—if indeed it ever can arrive.

As a matter of fact, however, for centuries past, in all parts of the world, we have had a class-state, with possessing classes on top and a propertyless laboring class at the bottom, even when population was much less dense than it is to-day. Now it is true that the class-state can arise only where all fertile acreage has been occupied completely; and since I have shown that even at the present time, all the ground is not occupied economically, this must mean that it has been preempted politically. Since land could not have acquired "natural scarcity," the scarcity must have been "legal." This means that the land has been preempted by a ruling class against its subject class, and settlement prevented. Therefore the State, as a class-state, can have originated in no other way than through conquest and subjugation.

This view, the so-called "sociologic idea of the state," as the following will show, is supported in ample manner by well-known historical facts. And yet most modern historians have rejected it, holding that both groups, amalgamated by war into one State, before that time had, each for itself formed a "State." As there is no method of obtaining historical proof to the contrary, since the beginnings of human history are unknown, we should arrive at a verdict of "not proven," were it not that, deductively, there is the absolute certainty that the State, as history shows it, the class-state, could not have come about except through warlike subjugation. The mass of evidence shows that our simple calculation excludes any other result.

Franz Oppenheimer

The Sociological Idea of the State: To the originally, purely sociological, idea of the State, I have added the economic phase and formulated it as follows:

What, then, is the State as a sociological concept? The State, completely in its genesis, essentially and almost completely during the first stages of its existence, is a social institution, forced by a victorious group of men on a defeated group, with the sole purpose of regulating the dominion of the victorious group over the vanquished, and securing itself against revolt from within and attacks from abroad. Teleologically, this dominion had no other purpose than the economic exploitation of the vanquished by the victors.

No primitive state known to history originated in any other manner. Wherever a reliable tradition reports otherwise, either it concerns the amalgamation of two fully developed primitive states into one body of more complete organization; or else it is an adaptation to men of the fable of the sheep which made a bear their king in order to be protected against the wolf. But even in this latter case, the form and content of the State became precisely the same as in those states where nothing intervened, and which became immediately "wolf states."

The little history learned in our school-days suffices to prove this generic doctrine. Everywhere we find some warlike tribe of wild men breaking through the boundaries of some less warlike people, settling down as nobility and founding its State. In Mesopotamia, wave follows wave, state follows state—Babylonians, Amoritans, Assyrians, Arabs, Medes, Persians, Macedonians, Parthians, Mongols, Seldshuks, Tartars, Turks; on the Nile, Hyksos, Nubians, Persians, Greeks, Romans, Arabs, Turks; in Greece, the Doric States are typical examples; in Italy, Romans, Ostrogoths, Lombards, Franks, Germans; in Spain, Carthaginians, Visigoths, Arabs; in Gaul, Romans, Franks, Burgundians, Normans; in Britain, Saxons, Normans. In India wave upon wave of wild warlike clans has flooded over the country even to the islands of the Indian Ocean. So also is it with China. In the European colonies, we find the selfsame type, wherever a settled element of the population has been found, as for example, in South America and Mexico. Where that element is lacking, where only roving huntsmen are found, who may be exterminated but not subjugated, the conquerors resort to the device of

125

importing from afar masses of men to be exploited, to be subject perpetually to forced labor, and thus the slave trade arises.

An apparent exception is found only in those European colonies in which it is forbidden to replace the lack of a domiciled indigenous population by the importation of slaves. One of these colonies, the United States of America, is among the most powerful state-formations in all history. The exception there found is to be explained by this, that the mass of men to be exploited and worked without cessation imports itself, by emigration in great hordes from primitive states or from those in higher stages of development in which exploitation has become unbearable, while liberty of movement has been attained. In this case, one may speak of an infection from afar with "statehood" brought in by the infected of foreign lands. Where, however, in such colonies, immigration is very limited, either because of excessive distances and the consequent high charges for moving from home, or because of regulations limiting the immigration, we perceive an approximation to the final end of the development of the State, which we nowadays recognize as the necessary outcome and finale, but for which we have not yet found a scientific terminology. Here again, in the dialectic development, a change in the quantity is bound up with a change of the quality. The old form is filled with new contents. We still find a "State" in so far as it represents the tense regulation, secured by external force, whereby is secured the social living together of large bodies of men; but it is no longer the "State" in its older sense. It is no longer the instrument of political domination and economic exploitation of one social group by another; it is no longer a "State of Classes." It rather resembles a condition which appears to have come about through a "social contract." This stage is approached by the Australian Colonies, excepting Queensland, which after the feudal manner still exploits the half enslaved Kanakas. It is almost attained in New Zealand.

So long as there is no general assent as to the origin and essence of states historically known or as to the sociological meaning of the word "State" it would be futile to attempt to force into use a new name for these most advanced commonwealths. They will continue to be called "states" in spite of all protests, especially because of the pleasure of using confusing concepts. For the purpose of this study, however, we propose to employ a new concept, a different verbal lever, and shall speak of the result of the new process as a "Freemen's Citizenship."

This summary survey of the states of the past and present should, if space permitted, be supplemented by an examination of the facts offered by the study of races, and of those states which are not treated in our falsely called "Universal History." On this point, the assurance may be accepted that here again our general rule is valid without exception. Everywhere, whether in the Malay Archipelago, or in the "great sociological laboratory of Africa," at all places on this planet where the development of tribes has at all attained a higher form, the State grew from the subjugation of one group of men by another. Its basic justification, its raison d'être, was and is the economic exploitation of those subjugated.

The summary review thus far made may serve as proof of the basic premise of this sketch. The pathfinder to whom, before all others, we are indebted for this line of investigation is Professor Ludwig Gumplowicz of Graz, jurist and sociologist, who crowned a brave life by a brave self-chosen death. We can, then, in sharp outlines, follow in the sufferings of humanity the path which the State has pursued in its progress through the ages.

Robert Michels
1876-1936

Source: *Political Parties* (1911)
Selection: "Final Considerations"

Introduction: *Robert Michels was a German sociologist born in Cologne to a bourgeois-patrician family with a German-French-Belgian background. His youth included attending the Gymnasium in Berlin, serving in the army, studying in England, France, and Munich, and completing his dissertation in history, in 1900. He then soon became a student of Max Weber (who showed great personal interest in Michels), and also spent time as a member of the German Socialist Party. This resulted in German universities denying him employment, a situation Weber found unacceptable, and led to Michels moving to Italy where, for a short while, he became a revolutionary syndicalist.*

In 1910, Michels finished his classic work, Political Parties, *which was published in 1911 and soon translated into Italian (1912) and English (1915). During this time, World War I broke out and Michels refused to support Germany, which caused a breach in his relationship with Weber. Michels then moved to Basel, in 1914, where he became professor of economics. Throughout the 1920s he taught at various universities in Rome, Perugia, and the United States.*

In his writings and social activism Michels—like many sociologists of his generation— was concerned with applying the sociological founders' insights to twentieth-century Western society. He therefore wrestled with problems such as democracy, revolution, nationalism, socialism, mass society, imperialism, and class conflict. Unlike some of his contemporaries, he also studied topics such as feminism, sex, and morality. He was especially attracted to revitalizing the labor movement by combining the ideas of theorists such as Marx and Pareto.

In his classic work Political Parties, *Michels analyzes the power structures of political parties, trade unions, and other organizations. His main argument is that all organizations, even those most committed to equality and democracy—including socialist political parties—are unavoidably dominated by a small group of leaders, i.e., they are oligarchic. His systematic analysis explains how radical political parties lose their idealistic goals when subjected to the process of electoral participation. According to Michels, oligarchies do not reflect leaders' personal flaws but, rather, result from the nature of social structures themselves, which require a division of labor to carry out organizational programs effectively and efficiently. Ultimately, Michels believed the only way there could be a complete solution to the oligarchical problem and the realization of democracy was for leaders to encourage open lines of communication and devote themselves fully to the concerns of others. In the final chapter of Political Parties, presented below, Michels concisely sums up his main points about the "iron law of oligarchy" and other impedments to realizing democratic ideals.*

*

Leadership is a necessary phenomenon in every form of social life. Consequently it is not the task of science to inquire whether this phenomenon is good or evil, or predominantly one or the other. But there is great scientific value in the demonstration that every system of leadership is incompatible with the most essential postulates of democracy. We are now aware that the law of the historic necessity of oligarchy is primarily based upon a series of facts of experience. Like all other scientific laws, sociological laws are derived from empirical observation. In order, however, to deprive our axiom of its purely descriptive character, and to confer upon it that status of analytical explanation which can alone transform a formula into a law, it does not suffice to contemplate from a unitary outlook those phenomena which may be empirically established; we must also study the determining causes of these phenomena. Such has been our task.

Now, if we leave out of consideration the tendency of the leaders to organize themselves and to consolidate their interests, and if we leave also out of consideration the gratitude of the led towards the leaders, and the general immobility and passivity of the masses, we are led to conclude that the principal cause of oligarchy in the democratic parties is to be found in the technical indispensability of leadership.

The process which has begun in consequence of the differentiation of functions in the party is completed by a complex of qualities which the leaders acquire through their detachment from the mass. At the outset, leaders arise spontaneously; their functions are *accessory* and *gratuitous*. Soon, however, they become professional leaders, and in this second stage of development they are *stable* and *irremovable*.

It follows that the explanation of the oligarchical phenomenon which thus results is partly psychological; oligarchy derives, that is to say, from the psychical transformations which the leading personalities in the parties undergo in the course of their lives. But also, and still more, oligarchy depends upon what we may term the psychology of organization itself, that is to say, upon the tactical and technical necessities which result from the consolidation of every disciplined political aggregate. Reduced to its most concise expression, the fundamental sociological law of political parties (the term "political" being here used in its most comprehensive significance) may be formulated in the following terms: "It is organization which gives birth to the dominion of the elected over the electors, of the mandataries over the mandators, of the delegates over the delegators. Who says organization, says oligarchy."

Every party organization represents an oligarchical power grounded upon a democratic basis. We find everywhere electors and elected. Also we find everywhere that the power of the elected leaders over the electing masses is almost unlimited. The oligarchical structure of the building suffocates the basic democratic principle. That which is oppresses that which ought to be. For the masses, this essential difference between the reality and the ideal remains a mystery. Socialists often cherish a sincere belief that a new elite of politicians will keep faith better than did the old. The notion of the representation of popular interests, a notion to which the great majority of democrats, and in especial the working-class masses of the German-speaking lands, cleave with so much tenacity and confidence, is an illusion engendered by a false illumination, is an effect of mirage. In one of the most delightful pages of his analysis of modern Don Quixotism, Alphonse Daudet shows us how the "brav commandant" Bravida, who has never quitted Tarascon, gradually comes to persuade himself, influenced by the burning southern sun, that he has been to Shanghai and has had all kinds of heroic adventures. Similarly the modern proletariat, enduringly influenced by glib-tongued persons intellectually superior to the mass, ends by believing that by flocking to the poll and entrusting its social and economic cause to a delegate, its direct participation in power will be assured.

130

Robert Michels

The formation of oligarchies within the various forms of democracy is the outcome of organic necessity, and consequently affects every organization, be it socialist or even anarchist. . . . The supremacy of the leaders in the democratic and revolutionary parties has to be taken into account in every historic situation present and to come, even though only a few and exceptional minds will be fully conscious of its existence. The mass will never rule except *in abstracto*. Consequently the question we have to discuss is not whether ideal democracy is realizable, but rather to what point and in what degree democracy is desirable, possible, and realizable at a given moment. In the problem as thus stated we recognize the fundamental problem of politics as a science. Whoever fails to perceive this must, as Sombart says, either be so blind and fanatical as not to see that the democratic current daily makes undeniable advance, or else must be so inexperienced and devoid of critical faculty as to be unable to understand that all order and all civilization must exhibit aristocratic features. The great error of socialists, an error committed in consequence of their lack of adequate psychological knowledge, is to be found in their combination of pessimism regarding the present, with rosy optimism and immeasurable confidence regarding the future. A realistic view of the mental condition of the masses shows beyond question that even if we admit the possibility of moral improvement in mankind, the human materials with whose use politicians and philosophers cannot dispense in their plans of social reconstruction are not of a character to justify excessive optimism. Within the limits of time for which human provision is possible, optimism will remain the exclusive privilege of Utopian thinkers.

The socialist parties, like the trade unions, are living forms of social life. As such they react with the utmost energy against any attempt to analyse their structure or their nature, as if it were a method of vivisection. When science attains to results which conflict with their apriorist ideology, they revolt with all their power. Yet their defence is extremely feeble. Those among the representatives of such organizations whose scientific earnestness and personal good faith make it impossible for them to deny outright the existence of oligarchical tendencies in every form of democracy, endeavour to explain these tendencies as the outcome of a kind of atavism in the mentality of the masses, characteristic of the youth of the movement. The masses, they assure us, are still infected by the oligarchic virus simply because they have been oppressed during long centuries of slavery, and have never yet enjoyed an autonomous existence. The socialist regime, however, will soon restore them to health, and will burnish them with all the capacity necessary for self-government. Nothing could be more anti-scientific than the supposition that as soon as socialists have gained possession of governmental power it will suffice for the masses to exercise a little control over their leaders to secure that the interests of these leaders shall coincide perfectly with the interests of the led. This idea may be compared with the view of Jules Guesde, no less anti-scientific than anti-Marxist (though Guesde proclaims himself a Marxist), that whereas Christianity has made God into a man, socialism will make man into a god.

The objective immaturity of the mass is not a mere transitory phenomenon which will disappear with the progress of democratization *au lendemain du socialism* [after socialism]. On the contrary, it derives from the very nature of the mass as mass, for this, even when organized, suffers from an incurable incompetence for the solution of the diverse problems which present themselves for solution—because the mass *per se* is amorphous, and therefore needs division of labour, specialization, and guidance. *"L'espece humaine veut etre gouvernee; elle le sera. J'ai honte de mon espece,"* ["The human species wants to be governed; it will be. I am ashamed of my species."] wrote Proudhon from his prison in 1850. Man as individual is by nature predestined to be guided, and to be guided all the more in proportion as the functions of life undergo division and subdivision. To an enormously greater degree is guidance necessary for the social group.

From this chain of reasoning and from these scientific convictions it would be erroneous to conclude that we should renounce all endeavours to ascertain the limits which may be imposed upon the powers exercised over the individual by oligarchies (state, dominant class, party, etc.). It would be an error to abandon the desperate enterprise of endeavouring to discover a social order which will render possible the complete realization of the idea of popular sovereignty. In the present work, as the writer said at the outset, it has not been his aim to indicate new paths. But it seemed necessary to lay considerable stress upon the pessimist aspect of democracy which is forced on us by historical study. We had to inquire whether, and within what limits, democracy must remain purely ideal, possessing no other value than that of a moral criterion which renders it possible to appreciate the varying degrees of that oligarchy which is immanent in every social regime. In other words, we have had to inquire if, and in what degree, democracy is an ideal which we can never hope to realize in practice. A further aim of this work was the demolition of some of the facile and superficial democratic illusions which trouble science and lead the masses astray. Finally, the author desired to throw light upon certain sociological tendencies which oppose the reign of democracy, and to a still greater extent oppose the reign of socialism.

The writer does not wish to deny that every revolutionary working-class movement, and every movement sincerely inspired by the democratic spirit, may have a certain value as contributing to the enfeeblement of oligarchic tendencies. The peasant in the fable, when on his death-bed, tells his sons that a treasure is buried in the field. After the old man's death the sons dig everywhere in order to discover the treasure. They do not find it. But their indefatigable labour improves the soil and secures for them a comparative well-being. The treasure in the fable may well symbolize democracy. Democracy is a treasure which no one will ever discover by deliberate search. But in continuing our search, in labouring indefatigably to discover the indiscoverable, we shall perform a work which will have fertile results in the democratic sense. We have seen, indeed, that within the bosom of the democratic working-class party are born the very tendencies to counteract which that party came into existence. Thanks to the diversity and to the unequal worth of the elements of the party, these tendencies often give rise to manifestations which border on tyranny. We have seen that the replacement of the traditional legitimism of the powers-that-be by the brutal plebiscitary rule of Bonapartist parvenus does not furnish these tendencies with any moral or aesthetic superiority. Historical evolution mocks all the prophylactic measures that have been adopted for the prevention of oligarchy. If laws are passed to control the dominion of the leaders, it is the laws which gradually weaken, and not the leaders. Sometimes, however, the democratic principle carries with it, if not a cure, at least a palliative, for the disease of oligarchy. When Victor Considérant formulated his "democratico-pacificist" socialism, he declared that socialism signified, not the rule of society by the lower classes of the population, but the government and organization of society in the interest of all, through the intermediation of a group of citizens; and he added that the numerical importance of this group must increase *pari passu* with social development. This last observation draws attention to a point of capital importance. It is, in fact, a general characteristic of democracy, and hence also of the labour movement, to stimulate and to strengthen in the individual the intellectual aptitudes for criticism and control. We have seen how the progressive bureaucratization of the democratic organism tends to neutralize the beneficial effects of such criticism and such control. None the less it is true that the labour movement, in virtue of the theoretical postulates it proclaims, is apt to bring into existence (in opposition to the will of the leaders) a certain number of free spirits who, moved by principle, by instinct, or by both, desire to revise the base upon which authority is established. Urged on by conviction or by temperament, they are never weary of asking an eternal "Why?" about every human institution. Now this predisposition towards free inquiry, in which we cannot fail to recognize one of the most precious factors of civilization, will gradually increase in proportion as the economic status of the masses undergoes improvement and becomes more stable, and in proportion as they are admitted more effectively to the advantages of civilization. A wider education involves an increasing capacity for exercising control. Can we not observe every day that among the well-to-do the authority of the leaders over the led, extensive though it be, is never so unrestricted as in the case of the leaders of the poor? Taking in the mass, the poor are powerless and disarmed *vis-a-vis* their leaders. Their intellectual and cultural inferiority makes it impossible for them to see whither the leader is going, or to estimate in advance the significance of his actions. It is, consequently, the great task of social education to raise the intellectual level of the masses, so that they may be enabled, within the limits of what is possible, to counteract the oligarchical tendencies of the working-class movement.

In view of the perennial incompetence of the masses, we have to recognize the existence of two regulative principles:

1. The *ideological* tendency of democracy towards criticism and control; 2. The *effective* counter-tendency of democracy towards the creation of parties ever more complex and ever more differentiated—

parties, that is to say, which are increasingly based upon the competence of the few.

To the idealist, the analysis of the forms of contemporary democracy cannot fail to be a source of bitter deceptions and profound discouragement. Those alone, perhaps, are in a position to pass a fair judgment upon democracy who, without lapsing into dilettantist sentimentalism, recognize that all scientific and human ideals have relative values. If we wish to estimate the value of democracy, we must do so in comparison with its converse, pure aristocracy. The defects inherent in democracy are obvious. It is none the less true that as a form of social life we must choose democracy as the least of evils. The ideal government would doubtless be that of an aristocracy of persons at once morally good and technically efficient. But where shall we discover such an aristocracy? We may find it sometimes, though very rarely, as the outcome of deliberate selection; but we shall never find it where the hereditary principle remains in operation. Thus monarchy in its pristine purity must be considered as imperfection incarnate, as the most incurable of ills; from the moral point of view it is inferior even to the most revolting of demagogic dictatorships, for the corrupt organism of the latter at least contains a healthy principle upon whose working we may continue to base hopes of social resanation. It may be said, therefore, that the more humanity comes to recognize the advantages which democracy, however imperfect, presents over aristocracy, even at its best, the less likely is it that a recognition of the defects of democracy will provoke a return to aristocracy. Apart from certain formal differences and from the qualities which can be acquired only by good education and inheritance (qualities in which aristocracy will always have the advantage over democracy—qualities which democracy either neglects altogether, or, attempting to imitate them, falsifies them to the point of caricature), the defects of democracy will be found to inhere in its inability to get rid of its aristocratic scoriae. On the other hand, nothing but a serene and frank examination of the oligarchical dangers of democracy will enable us to minimize these dangers, even though they can never be entirely avoided.

The democratic currents of history resemble successive waves. They break ever on the same shoal. They are ever renewed. This enduring spectacle is simultaneously encouraging and depressing. When democracies have gained a certain stage of development, they undergo a gradual transformation, adopting the aristocratic spirit, and in many cases also the aristocratic forms, against which at the outset they struggled so fiercely. Now new accusers arise to denounce the traitors; after an era of glorious combats and of inglorious power, they end by fusing with the old dominant class; whereupon once more they are in their turn attacked by fresh opponents who appeal to the name of democracy. It is probable that this cruel game will continue without end.

William F. Ogburn
1886-1959

Source: *Social Change with Respect to Culture and Original Nature* (1922)
Selection: "Social Maladjustments: The Hypothesis of Cultural Lag"

Introduction: *William Fielding Ogburn, an American sociologist born in Butler, GA, received his Master of Arts degree in 1909 and doctorate in 1912 in sociology from Columbia University. At that time, the faculty was concerned with statistical analysis and quantitative methodology, which affected Ogburn's approach to research and theory throughout his illustrious career. After graduation, Ogburn was a professor of sociology, both at Columbia University (from 1919 to 1927) and at the University of Chicago (from 1927 to 1951). He also held many important positions with the federal government, including director of research for the President's Research Committee on Social Trends (1930-1933), director of the Consumers Advisory Board of the National Recovery Administration (1933), and research consultant for the National Resources Committee (1935-1943). In addition, Ogburn was president of the American Sociological Association; president of the American Statistical Association, where he was also the editor of its journal; president of the Society for the History of Technology (which was founded in 1959, the year he died); a vice president of the American Association for the Advancement of Science; and chairman of the Social Science Research Council.*

During his career he also wrote several major books, including Social Change—*a classic of sociology—and the textbook* Sociology, *coauthored with Meyer Nimkoff, which has been revised several times since 1940. In 1951, Ogburn formally retired, but he continued to lecture abroad, at the universities of Calcutta and Delhi in India, and at Nuffield College, Oxford.*

Although Ogburn was a sociologist, he was highly interested in psychoanalysis and underwent such analysis himself. This perspective made him aware of the widespread bias among researchers, and led him to propose that social scientists should become aware of their own prejudices, rationalizations, and biases in order to eliminate emotions and hidden desires from their theories. Ogburn was also influenced by cultural anthropology, which made him focus more on cultural constructs and less on psychological factors derived from his experiences with psychoanalysis. Throughout his

137

William F. Ogburn

career, he emphasized the value of recognizing the interdependence of the various social science disciplines, which was reflected in his own work.

In particular, he was interested in problems related to social change, including the ability to describe and measure it. He initially formulated and analyzed such problems in Social Change *(1922), which contains the reading below. In that influential book, Ogburn introduced the concept of "culture lag," which generally refers to the gap between technical innovations and the subsequent changes that must be made in various aspects of culture, such as values, laws, and customs, to ensure adjustment rather than discrepancies in societies. Ogburn's clear, concise theory and model have been widely used to explain difficulties and resistances societies have in adjusting to social change.*

*

That this is an age of change is an expression frequently heard to-day. Never before in the history of mankind have so many and so frequent changes occurred. These changes, it should be observed, are in the cultural conditions. The climate is changing no more rapidly, and the geological processes affecting land and water distribution and altitude are going on with their usual slowness. Nor apparently is the biological nature of man undergoing more rapid changes than formerly. We know that biological man changes through mutations which occur very rarely indeed, and we have no biological evidence to show and little reason to think that mutations in mental or physical man are occurring more frequently now than in the past. These changes that we see taking place all about us are in that great cultural accumulation which is man's social heritage. It has already been shown that these cultural changes were in early times rather infrequent, but that in modern times they have been occurring faster and faster until today mankind is almost bewildered in his effort to keep adjusted to these ever-increasing social changes. This rapidity of social change may be due to the increase in inventions which in turn is made possible by the accumulative nature of material culture. These conclusions follow from the preceding analyses.

The Hypothesis of Cultural Lag: This rapidity of change in modern times raises the very important question of social adjustment. Problems of social adjustment are of two sorts. One concerns the adaptation of man to culture or perhaps preferably the adapting of culture to man. This subject is considered in Part V. The other problem is the question of adjustments, occasioned as a result of these rapid social changes, between the different parts of culture, which no doubt means ultimately the adaptation of culture to man. This second problem of adjustment between the different parts of culture is the immediate subject of our inquiry.

The thesis is that the various parts of modern culture are not changing at the same rate, some parts are changing much more rapidly than others; and that since there is a correlation and interdependence of parts, a rapid change in one part of our culture requires readjustments through other changes in the various correlated parts of culture. For instance, industry and education are correlated, hence a change in industry makes adjustments necessary through changes in the educational system. Industry and education are two variables, and if the change in industry occurs first and the adjustment through education follows, industry may be referred to as the independent variable and education as the dependent variable. Where one part of culture changes first, through some discovery or invention, and occasions changes in some part of culture dependent upon it, there frequently is a delay in the changes occasioned in the dependent part of culture. The extent of this lag will vary according to the nature of the cultural material, but may exist for a considerable number of years, during which time there may be said to be a maladjustment. It is desirable to reduce the period of maladjustment, to make the cultural adjustments as quickly as possible.

The foregoing account sets forth a problem that occurs when there is a rapid change in a culture of interdependent parts and when the rates of change in the parts are unequal. The discussion will be presented according to the following outlines. First the hypothesis will be presented, then examined and tested by a rather full consideration of the facts of a single instance, to be followed by several illustrations. Next the nature and cause of the phenomenon of cultural maladjustment in general will be analyzed. The extent of such cultural lags will be estimated, and finally the significance for society will be set forth.

A first simple statement of the hypothesis we wish to investigate now follows. A large part of our environment consists of the material conditions of life and a large part of our social heritage is our material culture. These material things consist of houses, factories, machines, raw materials, manufactured products, foodstuffs and other material objects. In using these material things we employ certain methods. Some of these methods are as simple as the technique of handling a tool. But a good many of the ways of using the material objects of culture involve rather larger usages and adjustments, such as customs, beliefs, philosophies, laws, governments. One important function of government, for instance, is the adjustment of the population to the material conditions of life, although there are other governmental functions. Sumner has called many of these processes of adjustments mores. The cultural adjustments to material conditions, however, include a larger body of processes than the mores; certainly they include the folkways and social institutions. These ways of adjustment may be called, for purposes of this particular analysis, the adaptive culture. The adaptive culture is therefore that portion of the non-material culture which is adjusted or adapted to the material conditions. Some parts of the non-material culture are thoroughly adaptive culture such as certain rules involved in handling technical appliances, and some parts are only indirectly or partially so, as for instance, religion. The family makes some adjustments to fit changed material conditions, while some of its functions remain constant. The family, therefore, under the terminology used here is a part of the non-material culture that is only partly adaptive. When the material conditions change, changes are occasioned in the adaptive culture. But these changes in the adaptive culture do not synchronize exactly with the change in the material culture. There is a lag which may last for varying lengths of time, sometimes indeed, for many years.

An illustration will serve to make the hypothesis more clearly understood. One class of material objects to which we adjust ourselves is the forests. The material conditions of forestry have changed a good deal in the United States during the past century. At one time the forests were quite plentiful for the needs of the small population. There was plenty of wood easily accessible for fuel, building and manufacture. The forests were sufficiently extensive to prevent in many large areas the washing of the soil, and the streams were clear. In fact, at one time the forests seemed to be too plentiful, from the point of view of the needs of the people. Food and agricultural products were at one time the first need of the people and the clearing of land of trees and stumps was a common undertaking of the community in the days of the early settlers. In some places, the quickest procedure was to kill and burn the trees and plant between the stumps. When the material conditions were like these, the method of adjustment to the forests was characterized by a policy which has been called exploitation. Exploitation in regard to the forests was indeed a part of the mores of the time, and describes a part of the adaptive culture in relation to forests.

As time went on, however, the population grew, manufacturing became highly developed, and the need for forests increased. But the forests were being destroyed. This was particularly true in the Appalachian, Great Lakes and Gulf regions. The policy of exploitation continued. Then rather suddenly it began to be realized in certain centres of thought that if the policy of cutting timber continued at the same rate and in the same manner the forests would in a short time be gone and very soon indeed they would be inadequate to supply the needs of the population. It was realized that the custom in regard to using the forests must be changed and a policy of conservation was advocated. The new policy of conservation means not only a restriction in the amount of cutting down of trees, but it means a more scientific method of cutting, and also reforestation. Forests may be cut in such a way, by selecting trees according to their size, age and location, as to yield a large quantity of timber and yet not diminish the forest area. Also by the proper distribution of cutting plots in a particular area, the cutting can be so timed that by the time the last plot is cut the young trees on the plot first cut will be grown. Some areas when cut leave a land which is well adapted to farming, whereas such sections as mountainous regions when denuded of forests are poorly suited to agriculture. There of course are many other methods of conservation of forests. The science of forestry is, indeed, fairly highly developed in principle, though not in practice in the United States. A new adaptive culture, one of conservation, is therefore suited to the changed material conditions.

That the conservation of forests in the United States should have been begun earlier is quite generally admitted. We may say, therefore, that the old policy of exploitation has hung over longer than it should before the institution of the new policy. In other words, the material conditions in regard to our forests have changed but the old customs of the use of forests which once fitted the material conditions very well have hung over into a period of changed conditions. These old customs are not only not satisfactorily adapted, but are really socially harmful. These customs of course have a utility, since they meet certain human needs; but methods of greater utility are needed. There seems to be a lag in the mores in regard to forestry after the material conditions have changed. Or translated into the general terms of the previous analysis, the material conditions have changed first; and there has been a lag in the adaptive culture, that is, that culture which is adapted to forests. The material conditions changed before the adaptive culture was changed to fit the new material conditions. . . .

The policy of conservation of forests certainly did not begin prior to 1904, when the first National Conservation Congress met. It was during Roosevelt's administration that many active steps in the direction of conservation were taken. Large areas of national forest lands were withdrawn from public entry. Gilford Pinchot was very active in spreading the gospel of conservation, and the House of Governors called by President Roosevelt was in large measure concerned with programmes of conservation. About this time many books and articles in magazines and periodicals were written on the subject. The conservation movement can hardly be said to have started in any extensive manner before this time. It is true that, earlier, papers had been read on the subject before scientific societies and there had been some teaching of scientific forestry, but prior to this time the idea of forest conservation was little known and the movement was certainly not extensive. Nor had the government taken any significant steps in a genuine policy of conservation. Indeed it might be argued with some success that we have not yet adopted fully a policy of conservation. For a great many of the private holdings are still exploited in very much the same old way. Reforestation is still largely a matter of theory in the United States. It is true that the government has taken a number of steps to preserve the forests but the conservationists are far from being satisfied with the progress of the movement to date. Certainly we have not attained the high mark maintained in Western Europe.

It is also difficult to . . . determine when we should have started the conservation movement. Some features of conservation probably should have been instituted perhaps early in the last century. Thus the allotment of permanent forest areas might very well have been done coincidently with the extension of our domain; and the destruction of forests on land little suited to agriculture might have been prevented as the population spread to these new regions. At the time of the Civil War the population had become quite large, and shortly afterward the era of railroad-building set in followed by a great development of industry, insuring large population and concentration. It was at this time that the wonderful forests of the Great Lakes region were cut down, and the cuttings in the Appalachian regions increased greatly. Some close observers saw at that time what development of population and industry would take place, but the relation of the forests to such a condition was not appreciated. If scientific forestry had been applied then, many of the unnecessarily wasted forests would still exist and now be furnishing lumber. There would not have been such a washing of soil and the danger of floods would have been less. While some methods of forest conservation might have been applied to advantage shortly after colonial days, the proper time for more extensive developments of conservation was probably in the era following the Civil War. The population was becoming large; the west was being settled; the Pacific coast had been reached; the territorial boundaries had been fixed; industries, railroads, factories, corporations, trusts were all growing with rapidity. The east was in greater need of conservation of forests than the Pacific Northwest or Alaska; nevertheless very probably for the whole country, though its stages of development were unequal, an extensive conservation movement should have been instituted about the middle of the last half of the nineteenth century. It would seem, therefore, that there has been a lag of at least a quarter of a century in changing our forestry policy.

The foregoing discussion of forestry illustrates the hypothesis which it is proposed to discuss. It is desirable to state more clearly and fully the points involved in the analysis. The first point concerns the degree of adjustment or correlation between the material conditions and the adaptive non-material culture. The degree of this adjustment may be only more or less perfect or satisfactory; but we do adjust ourselves to the material conditions through some form of culture; that is, we live, we get along, through this adjustment. The particular culture which is adjusted to the material conditions may be very complex, and, indeed, quite a number of widely different parts of culture may be adjusted to a fairly homogeneous material condition. Of a particular cultural form, such as the family or government, relationship to a particular material culture is only one of its purposes or functions. Not all functions of family organization, as, for instance, the affectional function, are primarily adaptive to material conditions.

Another point to observe is that the changes in the material culture precede changes in the adaptive culture. This statement is not in the form of a universal dictum. Conceivably, forms of adaptation might be worked out prior to a change in the material situation and the adaptation might be applied practically at the same time as the change in the material conditions. But such a situation presumes a very high degree of planning, prediction and control. The collection of data, it is thought, will show that at the present time there are a very large number of cases where the material conditions change and the changes in the adaptive culture follow later. There are certain general theoretical reasons why this is so; but it is not desirable to discuss these until later. For the present, the analysis will only concern those cases where changes in the adaptive culture do not precede changes in the material culture. Furthermore, it is not implied that changes may not occur in non-material culture while the material culture remains the same. Art or education, for instance, may undergo many changes with a constant material culture. Still another point in the analysis is that the old, unchanged, adaptive culture is not adjusted to the new, changed, material conditions. It may be true that the old adaptive culture is never wholly unadjusted to the new conditions. There may be some degree of adjustment. But the thesis is that the unchanged adaptive culture was more harmoniously related to the old than to the new material conditions and that a new adaptive culture will be better suited to the new material conditions than was the old adaptive culture. Adjustment is therefore a relative term, and perhaps only in a few cases would there be a situation which might be called perfect adjustment or perfect lack of adjustment.

W.E.B. Du Bois
1868-1963

Source: *The Souls of Black Folk* (1903)
Selection: "Of the Sons of Master and Man"

Introduction: *William Edward Burghardt Du Bois was an American sociologist, civil rights activist, educator, historian, and writer. Born and raised in Great Barrington, MA, he graduated as valedictorian of his high school in 1884, and then went on to receive the B.A. from Fisk University, in Nashville, and the M.A. in 1891 and the Ph.D. in 1895 in history from Harvard University (with a dissertation titled "The Suppression of the African Slave Trade to the United States of America, 1638-1870"). In 1896, he married Nina Gomer and they subsequently had two children. In 1896-97 Du Bois became assistant instructor in sociology at the University of Pennsylvania, where he conducted a pioneering sociological study of an urban community that was published as* The Philadelphia Negro: A Social Study *(1899). From 1897 to 1910, he was professor of economics and history at Atlanta University, where he also organized conferences and studies on the "Negro Problem" and edited or co-edited sixteen of the annual publications.*

In 1905 Du Bois, a lifelong socialist and communist, was one of the founders and the general secretary of the Niagara movement, an African American protest group of scholars and professionals; in 1909 he was one of the founders of the National Association for the Advancement of Colored People; and from 1910 to 1934 he was the NAACP's director of publicity and research, a member of the board of directors, and editor of Crisis, *its monthly magazine. In 1934 he resigned from the NAACP, which was committed to a strategy of integration, because he became impassioned with an African American nationalist strategy that championed African American control of institutions such as schools and economic cooperatives. In 1935, while chairman of the Department of Sociology at Atlanta University, Du Bois wrote* Black Reconstruction in America, 1860-1880 *(1935), an important historical work criticized by many for its use of Marxist concepts. In 1940, he founded* Phylon, *a social science quarterly.*

Du Bois returned to the NAACP from 1944 to 1948, as director of special research. During this period he was active in placing the grievances of African Americans before the United Nations, serving as a consultant to the UN founding convention (1945) and writing the famous "An Appeal to the World" (1947). In 1948, he co-chaired the Council on African Affairs; in 1949 he attended the peace congresses in New York, Paris, and Moscow; and in 1950 he ran for the U.S. Senate in New York, on the American Labor party ticket. In 1958-59, he traveled throughout Russia and China, and in 1961 he joined the Communist Party of the United States. In 1963, the year he died, he took up residence in Ghana, Africa, at the age of ninety-five, on the eve of the civil rights march in Washington, D.C.

Although Du Bois is iconic in his role as an African American leader, his most lasting contribution is his writing. In all, he wrote 21 books, edited 15 other books, and published over one hundred essays and articles. Throughout his life, all of his work and efforts were aimed at gaining blacks equal treatment relative to whites, and debunking claims of black racial inferiority. When he was a relatively young man, thirty-five years of age, he wrote The Souls of Black Folk: Essays and Sketches. *This book, which contains the following chapter, "Of the Sons of Master and Man," is generally considered among the most outstanding collections of essays in American letters.*

*

The world-old phenomenon of the contact of diverse races of men is to have new exemplification during the new century. Indeed, the characteristic of our age is the contact of European civilization with the world's undeveloped peoples. Whatever we may say of the results of such contact in the past, it certainly forms a chapter in human action not pleasant to look back upon. War, murder, slavery, extermination, and debauchery—this has again and again been the result of carrying civilization and the blessed gospel to the isles of the sea and the heathen without the law. Nor does it altogether satisfy the conscience of the modern world to be told complacently that all this has been right and proper, the fated triumph of strength over weakness, of righteousness over evil, of superiors over inferiors. It would certainly be soothing if one could readily believe all this; and yet there are too many ugly facts for everything to be thus easily explained away. We feel and know that there are many delicate differences in race psychology, numberless changes that our crude social measurements are not yet able to follow minutely, which explain much of history and social development. At the same time, too, we know that these considerations have never adequately explained or excused the triumph of brute force and cunning over weakness and innocence.

It is, then, the strife of all honorable men of the twentieth century to see that in the future competition of races the survival of the fittest shall mean the triumph of the good, the beautiful, and the true; that we may be able to preserve for future civilization all that is really fine and noble and strong, and not continue to put a premium on greed and impudence and cruelty. To bring this hope to fruition, we are compelled daily to turn more and more to a conscientious study of the phenomena of race-contact—to a study frank and fair, and not falsified and colored by our wishes or our fears. And we have in the South as fine a field for such a study as the world affords—a field, to be sure, which the average American scientist deems somewhat beneath his dignity, and which the average man who is not a scientist knows all about, but nevertheless a line of study which by reason of the enormous race complications with which God seems about to punish this nation must increasingly claim our sober attention, study, and thought, we must ask, what are the actual relations of whites and blacks in the South? And we must be answered, not by apology or fault-finding, but by a plain, unvarnished tale.

In the civilized life of to-day the contact of men and their relations to each other fall in a few main lines of action and communication: there is, first, the physical proximity of home and dwelling-places, the way in which neighborhoods group themselves, and the contiguity of neighborhoods. Secondly, and in our age chiefest, there are the economic relations—the methods by which individuals cooperate for earning a living, for the mutual satisfaction of wants, for the production of wealth. Next, there are the political relations, the cooperation in social control, in group government, in laying and paying the burden of taxation. In the fourth place there are the less tangible but highly important forms of intellectual contact and commerce, the interchange of ideas through conversation and conference, through periodicals and libraries; and, above all, the gradual formation for each community of that curious tertium quid which we call public opinion. Closely allied with this come the various forms of social contact in everyday life, in travel, in theatres, in house gatherings, in marrying and giving in marriage. Finally, there are the varying forms of religious enterprise, of moral teaching and benevolent endeavor. These are the principal ways in which men living in the same communities are brought into contact with each other. It is my present task, therefore, to indicate, from my point of view, how the black race in the South meet and mingle with the whites in these matters of everyday life.

First, as to physical dwelling. It is usually possible to draw in nearly every Southern community a physical color-line on the map, on the one side of which whites dwell and on the other Negroes. The winding and intricacy of the geographical color-line varies, of course, in different communities. I know some towns where a straight line drawn through the middle of the main street separates nine-tenths of the whites from nine-tenths of the blacks. In other towns the older settlement of whites has been encircled by a broad band of blacks; in still other cases little settlements or nuclei of blacks have sprung up amid surrounding whites. Usually in cities each street has its distinctive color, and only now and then do the colors meet in close proximity. Even in the country something of this segregation is manifest in the smaller areas, and of course in the larger phenomena of the Black Belt.

All this segregation by color is largely independent of that natural clustering by social grades common to all communities. A Negro slum may be in dangerous proximity to a white residence quarter, while it is quite common to find a white slum planted in the heart of a respectable Negro district. One thing, however, seldom occurs: the best of the whites and the best of the Negroes almost never live in anything like close proximity. It thus happens that in nearly every Southern town and city, both whites and blacks see commonly the worst of each other. This is a vast change from the situation in the past, when, through the close contact of master and house-servant in the patriarchal big house, one found the best of both races in close contact and sympathy, while at the same time the squalor and dull round of toil among the field-hands was removed from the sight and hearing of the family. One can easily see how a person who saw slavery thus from his father's parlors, and sees freedom on the streets of a great city, fails to grasp or comprehend the whole of the new picture. On the other hand, the settled belief of the mass of the Negroes that the Southern white people do not have the black man's best interests at heart has been intensified in later years by this continual daily contact of the better class of blacks with the worst representatives of the white race.

Coming now to the economic relations of the races, we are on ground made familiar by study, much discussion, and no little philanthropic effort. And yet with all this there are many essential elements in the cooperation of Negroes and whites for work and wealth that are too readily overlooked or not thoroughly understood. The average American can easily conceive of a rich land awaiting development and filled with black laborers. To him the Southern problem is simply that of making efficient workingmen out of this material, by giving them the requisite technical skill and the help of invested capital. The problem, however, is by no means as simple as this, from the obvious fact that these workingmen have been trained for centuries as slaves. They exhibit, therefore, all the advantages and defects of such training; they are willing and good-natured, but not self-reliant, provident, or careful. If now the economic development of the South is to be pushed to the verge of exploitation, as seems probable, then we have a mass of workingmen thrown into relentless competition with the workingmen of the world, but handicapped by a training the very opposite to that of the modern self-reliant democratic laborer. What the black laborer needs is careful personal guidance, group leadership of men with hearts in their bosoms, to train them to foresight, carefulness, and honesty. Nor does it require any fine-spun theories of racial differences to prove the necessity of such group training after the brains of the race have been knocked out by two hundred and fifty years of assiduous education in submission, carelessness, and stealing. After Emancipation, it was the plain duty of someone to assume this group leadership and training of the Negro laborer. I will not stop here to inquire whose duty it was—whether that of the white ex-master who had profited by unpaid toil, or the Northern philanthropist whose persistence brought on the crisis, or the National Government whose edict freed the bondmen; I will not stop to ask whose duty it was, but I insist it was the duty of someone to see that these workingmen were not left alone and unguided, without capital, without land, without skill, without economic organization, without even the bald protection of law, order, and decency—left in a great land, not to settle down to slow and careful internal development, but destined to be thrown almost immediately into relentless and sharp competition with the best of modern workingmen under an economic system where every participant is fighting for himself, and too often utterly regardless of the rights or welfare of his neighbor.

For we must never forget that the economic system of the South to-day which has succeeded the old regime is not the same system as that of the old industrial North, of England, or of France, with their trade unions, their restrictive laws, their written and unwritten commercial customs, and their long experience. It is, rather, a copy of that England of the early nineteenth century, before the factory acts—the England that wrung pity from thinkers and fired the wrath of Carlyle. The rod of empire that passed from the hands of Southern gentlemen in 1865, partly by force, partly by their own petulance, has never returned to them. Rather it has passed to those men who have come to take charge of the industrial exploitation of the New South—the sons of poor whites fired with a new thirst for wealth and power, thrifty and avaricious Yankees, and unscrupulous immigrants. Into the hands of these men the Southern laborers, white and black, have fallen; and this to their sorrow. For the laborers as such, there is in these new captains of industry neither love nor hate, neither sympathy nor romance; it is a cold question of dollars and dividends. Under such a system all labor is bound to suffer. Even the white laborers are not yet intelligent, thrifty, and well trained enough to maintain themselves against the powerful inroads of organized capital. The results among them, even, are long hours of toil, low wages, child labor, and lack of protection against usury and cheating. But among the black laborers all this is aggravated, first, by a race prejudice which varies from a doubt and distrust among the best element of whites to a frenzied hatred among the worst; and, secondly, it is aggravated, as I have said before, by the wretched economic heritage of the freedmen from slavery. With this training it is difficult for the freedman to learn to grasp the opportunities already opened to him, and the new opportunities are seldom given him, but go by favor to the whites.

Left by the best elements of the South with little protection or oversight, he has been made in law and custom the victim of the worst and most unscrupulous men in each community. The crop-lien system which is depopulating the fields of the South is not simply the result of shiftlessness on the part of Negroes, but is also the result of cunningly devised laws as to mortgages, liens, and misdemeanors, which can be made by conscienceless men to entrap and snare the unwary until escape is impossible, further toil a farce, and protest a crime. I have seen, in the Black Belt of Georgia, an ignorant, honest Negro buy and pay for a farm in installments three separate times, and then in the face of law and decency the enterprising American who sold it to him pocketed the money and deed and left the black man landless, to labor on his own land at thirty cents a day. I have seen a black farmer fall in debt to a white storekeeper, and that storekeeper go to his farm and strip it of every single marketable article—mules, ploughs, stored crops, tools, furniture, bedding, clocks, looking-glass—and all this without a sheriff or officer, in the face of the law for homestead exemptions, and without rendering to a single responsible person any account or reckoning. And such proceedings can happen, and will happen, in any community where a class of ignorant toilers are placed by custom and race-prejudice beyond the pale of sympathy and race-brotherhood. So long as the best elements of a community do not feel in duty bound to protect and train and care for the weaker members of their group, they leave them to be preyed upon by these swindlers and rascals.

This unfortunate economic situation does not mean the hindrance of all advance in the black South, or the absence of a class of black land-lords and mechanics who, in spite of disadvantages, are accumulating property and making good citizens. But it does mean that this class is not nearly so large as a fairer economic system might easily make it, that those who survive in the competition are handicapped so as to accomplish much less than they deserve to, and that, above all, the personnel of the successful class is left to chance and accident, and not to any intelligent culling or reasonable methods of selection. As a remedy for this, there is but one possible procedure. We must accept some of the race prejudice in the South as a fact—deplorable in its intensity, unfortunate in results, and dangerous for the future, but nevertheless a hard fact which only time can efface. We cannot hope, then, in this generation, or for several generations, that the mass of the whites can be brought to assume that close sympathetic and self-sacrificing leadership of the blacks which their present situation so eloquently demands. Such leadership, such social teaching and example, must come from the blacks themselves. For some time men doubted as to whether the Negro could develop such leaders; but to-day no one seriously disputes the capability of individual Negroes to assimilate the culture and common sense of modern civilization, and to pass it on, to some extent at least, to their fellows. If this is true, then here is the path out of the economic situation, and here is the imperative demand for trained Negro leaders of character and intelligence—men of skill, men of light and leading, college-bred men, black captains of industry, and missionaries of culture; men who thoroughly comprehend and know modern civilization, and can take hold of Negro communities and raise and train them by force of precept and example, deep sympathy, and the inspiration of common blood and ideals. But if such men are to be effective they must have some power— they must be backed by the best public opinion of these communities, and able to wield for their objects and aims such weapons as the experience of the world has taught are indispensable to human progress.

Of such weapons the greatest, perhaps, in the modern world is the power of the ballot; and this brings me to a consideration of the third form of contact between whites and blacks in the South—political activity.

In the attitude of the American mind toward Negro suffrage can be traced with unusual accuracy the prevalent conceptions of government. In the fifties we were near enough the echoes of the French Revolution to believe pretty thoroughly in universal suffrage. We argued, as we thought then rather logically, that no social class was so good, so true, and so disinterested as to be trusted wholly with the political destiny of its neighbors; that in every state the best arbiters of their own welfare are the persons directly affected; consequently that it is only by arming every hand with a ballot—with the right to have a voice in the policy of the state—that the greatest good to the greatest number could be attained. To be sure, there were objections to these arguments, but we thought we had answered them tersely and convincingly; if someone complained of the ignorance of voters, we answered, "Educate them." If another complained of their venality, we replied, "Disfranchise them or put them in jail." And, finally, to the men who feared demagogues and the natural perversity of some human beings we insisted that time and bitter experience would teach the most hardheaded. It was at this time that the question of Negro suffrage in the South was raised. Here was a defenceless people suddenly made free. How were they to be protected from those who did not believe in their freedom and were determined to thwart it? Not by force, said the North; not by government guardianship, said the South; then by the ballot, the sole and legitimate defence of a free people, said the Common Sense of the Nation. No one thought, at the time, that the ex-slaves could use the ballot intelligently or very effectively; but they did think that the possession of so great power by a great class in the nation would compel their fellows to educate this class to its intelligent use.

Meantime, new thoughts came to the nation: the inevitable period of moral retrogression and political trickery that ever follows in the wake of war overtook us. So flagrant became the political scandals that reputable men began to leave politics alone, and politics consequently became disreputable. Men began to pride themselves on having nothing to do with their own government, and to agree tacitly with those who regarded public office as a private perquisite. In this state of mind it became easy to wink at the suppression of the Negro vote in the South, and to advise self-respecting Negroes to leave politics entirely alone. The decent and reputable citizens of the North who neglected their own civic duties grew hilarious over the exaggerated importance with which the Negro regarded the franchise. Thus it easily happened that more and more the better class of Negroes followed the advice from abroad and the pressure from home, and took no further interest in politics, leaving to the careless and the venal of their race the exercise of their rights as voters. The black vote that still remained was not trained and educated, but further debauched by open and unblushing bribery, or force and fraud, until the Negro voter was thoroughly inoculated with the idea that politics was a method of private gain by disreputable means.

And finally, now, to-day, when we are awakening to the fact that the perpetuity of republican institutions on this continent depends on the purification of the ballot, the civic training of voters, and the raising of voting to the plane of a solemn duty which a patriotic citizen neglects to his peril and to the peril of his children's children—in this day, when we are striving for a renaissance of civic virtue, what are we going to say to the black voter of the South? Are we going to tell him still that politics is a disreputable and useless form of human activity? Are we going to induce the best class of Negroes to take less and less interest in government, and to give up their right to take such an interest, without a protest? I am not saying a word against all legitimate efforts to purge the ballot of ignorance, pauperism, and crime. But few have pretended that the present movement for disfranchisement in the South is for such a purpose; it has been plainly and frankly declared in nearly every case that the object of the disfranchising laws is the elimination of the black man from politics.

Now, is this a minor matter which has no influence on the main question of the industrial and intellectual development of the Negro? Can we establish a mass of black laborers and artisans and landholders in the South who, by law and public opinion, have absolutely no voice in shaping the laws under which they live and work? Can the modern organization of industry, assuming as it does free democratic government and the power and ability of the laboring classes to compel respect for their welfare—can this system be carried out in the South when half its laboring force is voiceless in the public councils and powerless in its own defence? To-day the black man of the South has almost nothing to say as to how much he shall be taxed, or how those taxes shall be expended; as to who shall execute the laws, and how they shall do it; as to who shall make the laws, and how they shall be made. It is pitiable that frantic efforts must be made at critical times to get law-makers in some States even to listen to the respectful presentation of the black man's side of a current controversy. Daily the Negro is coming more and more to look upon law and justice, not as protecting safeguards, but as sources of humiliation and oppression. The laws are made by men who have little interest in him; they are executed by men who have absolutely no motive for treating the black people with courtesy or consideration; and, finally, the accused law-breaker is tried, not by his peers, but too often by men who would rather punish ten innocent Negroes than let one guilty one escape.

I should be the last one to deny the patent weaknesses and shortcomings of the Negro people; I should be the last to withhold sympathy from the white South in its efforts to solve its intricate social problems. I freely acknowledged that it is possible, and sometimes best, that a partially undeveloped people should be ruled by the best of their stronger and better neighbors for their own good, until such time as they can start and fight the world's battles alone. I have already pointed out how sorely in need of such economic and spiritual guidance the emancipated Negro was, and I am quite willing to admit that if the representatives of the best white Southern public opinion were the ruling and guiding powers in the South to-day the conditions indicated would be fairly well fulfilled. But the point I have insisted upon and now emphasize again, is that the best opinion of the South to-day is not the ruling opinion. That to leave the Negro helpless and without a ballot to-day is to leave him not to the guidance of the best, but rather to the exploitation and debauchment of the worst; that this is no truer of the South than of the North—of the North than of Europe: in any land, in any country under modern free competition, to lay any class of weak and despised people, be they white, black, or blue, at the political mercy of their stronger, richer, and more resourceful fellows, is a temptation which human nature seldom has withstood and seldom will withstand. . . .

But after all that has been said on these more tangible matters of human contact, there still remains a part essential to a proper description of the South which it is difficult to describe or fix in terms easily understood by strangers. It is, in fine, the atmosphere of the land, the thought and feeling, the thousand and one little actions which go to make up life. In any community or nation it is these little things which are most elusive to the grasp and yet most essential to any clear conception of the group life taken as a whole. What is thus true of all communities is peculiarly true of the South, where, outside of written history and outside of printed law, there has been going on for a generation as deep a storm and stress of human souls, as intense a ferment of feeling, as intricate a writhing of spirit, as ever a people experienced. Within and without the sombre veil of color vast social forces have been at work—efforts for human betterment, movements toward disintegration and despair, tragedies and comedies in social and economic life, and a swaying and lifting and sinking of human hearts which have made this land a land of mingled sorrow and joy, of change and excitement and unrest.

The centre of this spiritual turmoil has ever been the millions of black freedmen and their sons, whose destiny is so fatefully bound up with that of the nation. And yet the casual observer visiting the South sees at first little of this. He notes the growing frequency of dark faces as he rides along—but otherwise the days slip lazily on, the sun shines, and this little world seems as happy and contented as other worlds he has visited. Indeed, on the question of questions—the Negro problem—he hears so little that there almost seems to be a conspiracy of silence; the morning papers seldom mention it, and then usually in a far-fetched academic way, and indeed almost everyone seems to forget and ignore the darker half of the land, until the astonished visitor is inclined to ask if after all there IS any problem here. But if he lingers long enough there comes the awakening: perhaps in a sudden whirl of passion which leaves him gasping at its bitter intensity; more likely in a gradually dawning sense of things he had not at first noticed. Slowly but surely his eyes begin to catch the shadows of the color-line: here he meets crowds of Negroes and whites; then he is suddenly aware that he cannot discover a single dark face; or again at the close of a day's wandering he may find himself in some strange assembly, where all faces are tinged brown or black, and where he has the vague, uncomfortable feeling of the stranger. He realizes at last that silently, resistlessly, the world about flows by him in two great streams: they ripple on in the same sunshine, they approach and mingle their waters in seeming carelessness—then they divide and flow wide apart. It is done quietly; no mistakes are made, or if one occurs, the swift arm of the law and of public opinion swings down for a moment, as when the other day a black man and a white woman were arrested for talking together on Whitehall Street in Atlanta.

Now if one notices carefully one will see that between these two worlds, despite much physical contact and daily intermingling, there is almost no community of intellectual life or point of transference where the thoughts and feelings of one race can come into direct contact and sympathy with the thoughts and feelings of the other. Before and directly after the war, when all the best of the Negroes were domestic servants in the best of the white families, there were bonds of intimacy, affection, and sometimes blood relationship, between the races. They lived in the same home, shared in the family life, often attended the same church, and talked and conversed with each other. But the increasing civilization of the Negro since then has naturally meant the development of higher classes: there are increasing numbers of ministers, teachers, physicians, merchants, mechanics, and independent farmers, who by nature and training are the aristocracy and leaders of the blacks. Between them, however, and the best element of the whites, there is little or no intellectual commerce. They go to separate churches, they live in separate sections, they are strictly separated in all public gatherings, they travel separately, and they are beginning to read different papers and books. To most libraries, lectures, concerts, and museums, Negroes are either not admitted at all, or on terms peculiarly galling to the pride of the very classes who might otherwise be attracted. The daily paper chronicles the doings of the black world from afar with no great regard for accuracy; and so on, throughout the category of means for intellectual communication—schools, conferences, efforts for social betterment, and the like—it is usually true that the very representatives of the two races, who for mutual benefit and the welfare of the land ought to be in complete understanding and sympathy, are so far strangers that one side thinks all whites are narrow and prejudiced, and the other thinks educated Negroes dangerous and insolent. Moreover, in a land where the tyranny of public opinion and the intolerance of criticism is for obvious historical reasons so strong as in the South, such a situation is extremely difficult to correct. The white man, as well as the Negro, is bound and barred by the color-line, and many a scheme of friendliness and philanthropy, of broad-minded sympathy and generous fellowship between the two has dropped still-born because some busybody has forced the color-question to the front and brought the tremendous force of unwritten law against the innovators.

It is hardly necessary for me to add very much in regard to the social contact between the races. Nothing has come to replace that finer sympathy and love between some masters and house servants which the radical and more uncompromising drawing of the color-line in recent years has caused almost completely to disappear. In a world where it means so much to take a man by the hand and sit beside him, to look frankly into his eyes and feel his heart beating with red blood; in a world where a social cigar or a cup of tea together means more than legislative halls and magazine articles and speeches—one can imagine the consequences of the almost utter absence of such social amenities between estranged races, whose separation extends even to parks and streetcars.

Here there can be none of that social going down to the people—the opening of heart and hand of the best to the worst, in generous acknowledgment of a common humanity and a common destiny. On the other hand, in matters of simple almsgiving, where there can be no question of social contact, and in the succor of the aged and sick, the South, as if stirred by a feeling of its unfortunate limitations, is generous to a fault.

The black beggar is never turned away without a good deal more than a crust, and a call for help for the unfortunate meets quick response. I remember, one cold winter, in Atlanta, when I refrained from contributing to a public relief fund lest Negroes should be discriminated against, I afterward inquired of a friend: "Were any black people receiving aid?" "Why," said he, "they were all black."

And yet this does not touch the kernel of the problem. Human advancement is not a mere question of almsgiving, but rather of sympathy and cooperation among classes who would scorn charity. And here is a land where, in the higher walks of life, in all the higher striving for the good and noble and true, the color-line comes to separate natural friends and coworkers; while at the bottom of the social group, in the saloon, the gambling-hall, and the brothel, that same line wavers and disappears.

I have sought to paint an average picture of real relations between the sons of master and man in the South. I have not glossed over matters for policy's sake, for I fear we have already gone too far in that sort of thing. On the other hand, I have sincerely sought to let no unfair exaggerations creep in. I do not doubt that in some Southern communities conditions are better than those I have indicated; while I am no less certain that in other communities they are far worse.

Nor does the paradox and danger of this situation fail to interest and perplex the best conscience of the South. Deeply religious and intensely democratic as are the mass of the whites, they feel acutely the false position in which the Negro problems place them. Such an essentially honest-hearted and generous people cannot cite the caste-levelling precepts of Christianity, or believe in equality of opportunity for all men, without coming to feel more and more with each generation that the present drawing of the color-line is a flat contradiction to their beliefs and professions. But just as often as they come to this point, the present social condition of the Negro stands as a menace and a portent before even the most open-minded: if there were nothing to charge against the Negro but his blackness or other physical peculiarities, they argue, the problem would be comparatively simple; but what can we say to his ignorance, shiftlessness, poverty, and crime? Can a self-respecting group hold anything but the least possible fellowship with such persons and survive? And shall we let a mawkish sentiment sweep away the culture of our fathers or the hope of our children? The argument so put is of great strength, but it is not a whit stronger than the argument of thinking Negroes: granted, they reply, that the condition of our masses is bad; there is certainly on the one hand adequate historical cause for this, and unmistakable evidence that no small number have, in spite of tremendous disadvantages, risen to the level of American civilization. And when, by proscription and prejudice, these same Negroes are classed with and treated like the lowest of their people, simply because they are Negroes, such a policy not only discourages thrift and intelligence among black men, but puts a direct premium on the very things you complain of—inefficiency and crime. Draw lines of crime, of incompetency, of vice, as tightly and uncompromisingly as you will, for these things must be proscribed; but a color-line not only does not accomplish this purpose, but thwarts it. . . .

It is not enough for the Negroes to declare that color-prejudice is the sole cause of their social condition, nor for the white South to reply that their social condition is the main cause of prejudice. They both act as reciprocal cause and effect, and a change in neither alone will bring the desired effect. Both must change, or neither can improve to any great extent. The Negro cannot stand the present reactionary tendencies and unreasoning drawing of the color-line indefinitely without discouragement and retrogression. And the condition of the Negro is ever the excuse for further discrimination. Only by a union of intelligence and sympathy across the color-line in this critical period of the Republic shall justice and right triumph,

> "That mind and soul according well,
> May make one music as before,
> But vaster."

References

Addams, Jane. 1902. *Democracy and Social Ethics*. London: Macmillan & Co. Selection: From Chapter III: "Filial Relations," pp. 71-101.

Bagehot, Walter. 1872. *Physics and Politics*. London: Henry S. King & Company. Retrieved from Project Gutenberg at http://www.gutenberg.org/files/4350/4350-h/4350-h.htm. Selection: From Chapter VI: "Verifiable Progress Politically Considered," unpaginated.

Du Bois, W.E.B. 1903. *The Souls of Black Folk*. Retreived from Project Gutenberg at http://www.gutenberg.org/files/408/408-h/408-h.htm. Selection: From Chapter IX: "Of the Sons of Master and Man," unpaginated.

Engels, Frederick. 1884 [1908]. *The Origin of the Family, Private Property and the State*. Retrieved from http://www.gutenberg.org/files/33111/33111-h/33111-h.htm#Page_176. Translated by Ernest Untermann. 1908. Chicago: Charles H. Kerr & Company. Selection: From Chapter IX: "Barbarism and Civilization," pp. 191-217.

Gilman, Charlotte Perkins. 1898. *Women and Economics*: *A Study of the Economic Relation between Men and Women as a Factor in Social Evolution*. Boston: Small, Maynard & Co. Selection: From Chapter VI: pp. 99-121. Note: The publisher lists her last name "Stetson," her married name.

Gumplowicz, Ludwig. 1899. *The Outlines of Sociology*. Philadelphia, PA: The American Academy of Political and Social Science. Translated by Frederick W. Moore. Selections: From Part II: "Concept, Function, Scope and Importance of Sociology," pp. 82-92 and Part III: "The State," pp.116-123.

Maine, Henry Sumner. 1861[1917]. *Ancient Law: Its Connection with the Early History of Society and its Relation to Modern Ideas*. London: J. M. Dent & Sons, Ltd. 1917. Retrieved from http://www.gutenberg.org/files/22910/22910-h/22910-h.htm#CHAPTER_II. Selections: From Chapter II: "Legal Fictions," pp. 14-26 and Chapter IX: "The Early History of Contract," pp. 180-216.

Martineau, Harriet. 1838. *How to Observe Morals and Manners.* London: Charles Knight and Company. Retrieved from http://www.gutenberg.org/files/33944/33944-h/33944-h.htm. Selection: From Part II, Chapter III: "Marriage and Woman," pp. 167-180.

Michels, Robert. 1911[1915]. *Political Parties: A Sociological Study of the Oligarchical Tendencies of Modern Democracy.* New York: Hearst's International Library Company. Translated by Eden and Cedar Paul. 1915. Selections: From Part Six, Chapter IV: "Final Considerations," pp. 400-408.

Ogburn, William F. 1922. *Social Change with Respect to Culture and Original Nature.* New York: B. W. Huebsch, Inc. Selection: From Part IV: "Social Maladjustments, The Hypothesis of Cultural Lag," pp. 199-212.

Oppenheimer, Franz. 1914. *The State: Its History and Development Viewed Sociologically.* New York: Vanguard Press. Translated by John M. Gitterman. Selection: From Chapter I: "The State," pp. 1-21.

Pareto, Vilfredo. 1916 [1935]. *The Mind and Society.* Retrieved from http://www.archive.org/stream/mindsocietytratt01pare/mindsocietyt ratt01pare_djvu.txt. 1935), Translated by Andrew Bongiorno and Arthur Livingston. 1935. New York: Harcourt Brace. Selection: From Volume I, Book I, Chapter I: "The Scientific Approach," pp. 1-12.

Park, Robert E. 1915. "The City: Suggestions for the Investigation of Human Behavior in the City Environment." *American Journal of Sociology, vol. XX* (5) pp. 577-612. Selection: From Sections I: "The City Plan and Local Organization," pp. 578-584 and "IV: "Temperment and the Urban Environment," pp. 607-12.

Ratzenhofer, Gustav. 1907 [1908]. *Sociology.* Leipzig: F. A. Brockhaus. Translated by Albion Small. 1908. "Ratzenhofer's Sociology," In *The American Journal of Sociology, vol. XIII* (4), Selection: "Introduction," pp. 433-438.

Small, Albion W. 1905. *General Sociology: An Exposition of the Main Development in Sociological Theory from Spencer to Ratzenhofer.* Chicago: The University of Chicago Press. Selection: From Chapter I, "The Subject Matter of Sociology," pp. 3-22.

Webb, Beatrice Potter. 1904. *The Cooperative Movement in Great Britain.* New York: Charles Scribner's Sons. Retrieved from https://archive.org/stream/cooperativemov00webb/cooperativemov00webb_djvu.txt. Selection: From Chapter VIII, "Conclusions," pp. 221-239.

Additional Recommended Books, Articles and Websites

Many print and electronic sources are devoted to the founders of sociology and their writings. Below are a few to help you further explore this area of study. Some of these sources contain extensive bibliographies, and the websites have links to other sites you will find of great value.

Books and Articles

Abraham, Joseph Hayim. 1977. *Origins and Growth of Sociology.* New York: Penguin Books.

Albrow, Martin. 1990. *Max Weber's Construction of Social Theory.* Houndmills: Macmillan.

Alexander, Jeffrey C. 1982. *The Antinomies of Classical Thought: Marx and Durkheim.* Berkeley: University of California Press.

———. 1988. *Durkheimian Sociology: Cultural Studies.* New York: Cambridge University Press.

Altschuler, Richard (Ed.). 2010. *Seminal Sociological Writings: From Auguste Comte to Max Weber.* New York: Gordian Knot Books.

Altschuler, Richard (Ed.). 2001. *The Living Legacy of Marx, Durkheim & Weber: Applications and Analyses of Classical Sociological Theory by Modern Social Scientists.* New York: Gordian Knot Books.

Andreski, Stanislav. 1984. *Max Weber's Insights and Errors.* London: Routledge and Kegan Paul.

Aron, Raymond. 1998. *Main Currents in Sociological Thought.* Piscataway, NJ: Transaction Publishers.

Atoji, Yoshio. 1984. *Sociology at the Turn of the Century.* Tokyo: Dobunkan.

Barnes, Harrry Elmer (Ed.). 1948. *An Introduction to the History of Sociology*. Chicago: Unversity of Chicago Press.

Beetham, David. 1985. *Max Weber and the Theory of Modern Politics*. Cambridge: Polity.

Bellah, Robert N. 1959. "Durkheim and History." *American Sociological Review, vol. 24*, no. 4 (August): 447–461.

Bendix, Reinhard. 1960. *Max Weber: An Intellectual Portrait*. Garden City, NY: Doubleday.

Bogardus, Emory S. 1922. *A History of Social Thought*. Los Angeles: University of Southern California Press.

Bologh, Roslyn Wallach. 1984. "Max Weber and the Dilemma of Rationality." In *Max Weber's Political Sociology*, ed. Ronald M. Glassman and Vatro Murvar, pp. 175–184. Westport, CT: Greenwood.

Borgatta, Edgar F. and Henry J. Meyer (Eds.). 1956. *Sociological Theory: Present Day Sociology from the Past*. New York: Alfred A. Knopf.

Bottomore, Tom. 1981. "A Marxist Consideration of Durkheim." *Social Forces, vol. 59*, no. 4 (June): 902–917.

Bottomore, Tom, and Robert Nisbet. 1978. "Structuralism." In *History of Sociological Analysis*, eds. Tom Bottomore and Robert Nisbet, pp. 557–599. New York: Basic Books.

Brubaker, Rogers. 1984. *The Limits of Rationality: An Essay on the Social and Moral Thought of Max Weber*. London: Allen and Unwin.

Buckley, Walter. 1967. *Sociology and Modern Systems Theory*. New York: Dryden.

Burger, Thomas. 1977. "Max Weber, Interpretive Sociology, and the Sense of Historical Science: A Positivistic Conception of Verstehen," *Sociological Quarterly 18* (Spring): 165–175.

———. 1985. "Power and Stratification: Max Weber and Beyond." In *Theory of Liberty, Legitimacy and Power*, ed. Vatro Murvar. Boston: Routledge and Kegan Paul.

Calhoun, Craig (Ed.). 2007. *Sociology in America: A History*. Chicago: University of Chicago Press.

Coleman, James S. 1990. *Foundations of Social Theory*. Cambridge: Harvard University Press.

Collins, Randall. 1986. *Weberian Sociological Theory*. Cambridge: Cambridge University Press.

————. 1994. *Four Sociological Traditions*. New York: Oxford University Press.

Comte, Auguste. 1896. *The Positive Philosophy of Auguste Comte*. 3 vols. London: Bell.

Cooley, Charles Horton. 1956. *The Two Major Works of Charles H. Cooley: Social Organization, Human Nature and the Social Order*. Glencoe, IL: Free Press.

Cormack, Patricia. 1996. "The Paradox of Durkheim's Manifesto: Reconsidering 'The Rules of Sociological Method.'" *Theory and Society, vol. 25*, issue 1 (February): 85–104.

Coser, Lewis A. 1977. *Masters of Sociological Thought*. New York: Harcourt Brace Jovanovich.

Craib, Ian. 1997. *Classical Social Theory*. New York: Oxford.

Durkheim, Emile. 1951. *Suicide*. New York: Free Press.

Eisenstadt, S. N. 1968. "Introduction." In *Max Weber on Charisma and Institution Building*, ed. S. N. Eisenstadt, pp. ix–xvi. Chicago: University of Chicago Press.

Emirbayer, Mustafa. 1996. "Useful Durkheim." *Sociological Theory, vol. 3* (July): 109–130.

Fenton, Steve, with Robert Reiner and Ian Hamnett. 1984. *Durkheim and Modern Sociology*. New York: Cambridge University Press.

Fletcher, Ronald. 1980. *The Making of Sociology: A Study of Sociological Theory*. New York: Macmillan.

Gerth, H. H. and C. Wright Mills. 1946. "Introduction." In *Essays from Max Weber*, ed. H. H. Gerth and C. Wright Mills, pp. 3–75. New York: Oxford.

Giddens, Anthony. 1979. *Émile Durkheim*. New York: Penguin.

Giddings, Franklin Henry. 1896. *The Principles of Sociology*. New York: Macmillan.

Gouldner, Alvin W. 1976. *The Dialectic of Ideology and Technology*. New York: Seabury.

Halsey, A. H. 2004. *A History of Sociology in Britain: Science, Literature, and Society*. Oxford: Oxford University Press.

Hennis, Wilhelm. 1983. "Max Weber's 'Central Question.'" *Economy and Society vol. 12*, no. 2:135–180.

Hindess, Barry. 1987. "Rationality and the Characterization of Modern Society." In *Max Weber, Rationality and Modernity*, eds. Sam Whimster and Scott Lash, pp. 137-53. London: Allen and Unwin.

Hinkle, Roscoe C., Jr. 1960. "Durkheim in American Sociology." In *Émile Durkheim, 1858–1917*, ed. Kurt H. Wolff, pp. 267–295. Columbus: Ohio State University Press.

Hofstadter, Richard. 1955. *Social Darwinism in America*. Revised edition. Boston: Beacon Press.

Horowitz, Irving Louis. 1972. *Foundations of Political* Sociology. New Jersey: Transaction Publishers.

House, Floyd Nelson. 1936. *The Development of Sociology*. New York: McGraw-Hill.

Huff, Toby E. 1984. *Max Weber and the Methodology of the Social Sciences*. New Brunswick, NJ: Transaction Books.

Ibn Khaldûn. 1958. *The Muqaddimah: An Introduction to History, vol. 2*, 2nd ed. Bollingen Series 43. Princeton: Princeton University Press.

Jones, Susan Stedman. 2001. *Durkheim Reconsidered*. Cambridge: Polity.

Kellner, Douglas. 1985. "Critical Theory, Max Weber, and the Dialectics of Domination." In *A Marx-Weber Dialogue*, eds. R. Antonio and R. Glassman, pp. 89–116. Lawrence: University Press of Kansas.

Keynes, Richard. 1983. "Malthus and Biological Equilibria." In *Malthus Past and Present*, eds. J. Dupaquier, A. Fauve-Chamoux, and E. Grebenik, pp. 359–364. New York: Academic Press.

LeBon, Gustave. 1960. *The Crowd*. New York: Viking.

Lengermann, Particia Madoo and Niebrugge-Brantley, Jill. (Eds.). 1997. *The Women Founders: Sociology and Social Theory, 1830-1930: A Text/Reader*. Boston: McGraw-Hill.

Lenski, Gerhard E. 1975. "Social Structure in Evolutionary Perspective." In *Approaches to the Study of Social Structure*, ed. Peter M. Blau. New York: Free Press.

Levine, Donald N. 1981. "Rationality and Freedom: Weber and Beyond." *Sociological Inquiry, vol. 51*, no. 1:5–25.

Lindholm, Charles. 1990. *Charisma*. Cambridge: Basil Blackwell.

Lukes, Steven. 1975. *Émile Durkheim: His Life and Work*. New York: Peregrine Books.

Lundberg, George A. 1939. *Foundations of Sociology*. New York: Macmillan.

Lyman, Stanford. 1984. "The Science of History and the Theory of Social Change." In *Max Weber's Political Sociology*, eds. Ronald M. Glassman and Vatro Murvar, pp. 189–199. Westport, CT: Greenwood.

Malthus, Thomas Robert. 1966. *First Essay on Population*. New York: Macmillan.

Mannheim, Karl. 1955. *Ideology and Utopia*. New York: Harvest Books.

Marcuse, Herbert. 1971. "Industrialization and Capitalism." In *Max Weber and Sociology Today*, ed. Otto Stammer, pp. 133–151. New York: Harper and Row.

Marks, Stephen R. 1974. "Durkheim's Theory of Anomie." *American Journal of Sociology, vol. 80*, no. 2: 329–363.

Martindale, Don. 1960. *The Nature and Types of Sociological Theory.* Boston: Houghton Mifflin Company.

Marx, Karl. 1922. *Das Kapital.* Hamburg, Germany: Meissner.

———. 1964. *Economic and Philosophic Manuscripts of 1844.* New York: International.

———. 1967. *Capital*, 3 vols., unabridged. New York: International.

Marx, Karl, and Friedrich Engels. 1969. *Selected Works*, 3 vols. Moscow: Progress.

McIntosh, Ian (Ed.) 1997. *Classical Sociological Theory: A Reader.* Edinburgh, Scotland: Edinburgh University Press.

Mead, George Herbert. 1962. *Mind, Self, and Society.* Chicago: University of Chicago Press.

Merton, Robert K. 1957. *Social Theory and Social Structure*, revised and enlarged edition. Glencoe, IL: Free Press.

———. 1973. *The Sociology of Science.* Chicago: University of Chicago Press.

Mommsen, Wolfgang J. 1974. *The Age of Bureaucracy: Perspectives on the Political Sociology of Max Weber.* Oxford: Basil Blackwell.

Naegele, Kaspar D. 1958. "Attachment and Alienation: Complementary Aspects of the Work of Durkheim and Simmel." *American Journal of Sociology, vol. 63*, no. 6 (May): 580–589.

Nisbet, Robert A. 1966. *The Sociological Tradition.* London: Heinemann.

Nozick, Robert. 1993. *The Nature of Rationality.* Princeton: Princeton University Press.

Orum, Anthony M. 1988. "Political Sociology." In *Handbook of Sociology*, ed. Neil J. Smelser. Berkeley: Sage.

Parkin, Frank. 1982. *Max Weber.* Chichester, UK: Ellis Horwood.

Parsons, Talcott. 1937. *The Structure of Social Action.* Glencoe, IL.: Free Press.

———. 1960. "Durkheim's Contribution to the Theory of Integration of Social Systems." In *Émile Durkheim, 1858–1917*, ed. Kurt H. Wolff, pp. 118–153. Columbus: Ohio State University Press.

———. 1961. (Ed.) *Theories of Society: Foundations of Modern Sociological Theory*. New York: Free Press.

Pope, Whitney. 1976. *Durkheim's Suicide: A Classic Analyzed*. Chicago: University of Chicago Press.

Popper, Karl R. 1961. *The Logic of Scientific Discovery*. New York: Science Editions.

Rawls, Anne Warfield. 1996. "Durkheim's Epistemology: The Neglected Argument." *American Journal of Sociology, vol. 102*, no. 2 (September): 430–482.

Ritzer, George. (2007). *Classical Sociological Theory, 5ᵗʰ Edition*. NY: McGraw-Hill.

Ritzer, George, and Richard Bell. 1981. "Émile Durkheim: Exemplar for an Integrated Sociological Paradigm?" *Social Forces, vol. 59*, no. 4 (June): 966–995.

Sayer, Derek. 1991. *Capitalism and Modernity: An Excursus on Marx and Weber*. London: Routledge.

Schluchter, Wolfgang. 1989. *Rationalism, Religion, and Domination: A Weberian Perspective*. Berkeley: University of California Press.

Schroeder, Ralph. 1992. *Max Weber and the Sociology of Culture*. Hawthorne, NY: Aldine.

Segady, Thomas W. 1987. *Value, Neo-Kantianism and the Development of Weberian Methodology*. New York: Peter Lang.

Simmel, Georg. 1950. *The Sociology of Georg Simmel*. Glencoe, IL: Free Press.

Smith, Adam. 1937. *An Inquiry into the Nature and Causes of the Wealth of Nations*. New York: Modern Library.

Sorokin, Pitirim. 1928. *Contemporary Sociological Theories*. New York: Harper.

Spencer, Herbert. 1898. *The Principles of Sociology*. 3 vols. New York: Appleton.

————. 1961. *The Study of Sociology*. Ann Arbor: University of Michigan Press.

Tekla, Tendzin N., and Whitney Pope. 1985. "The Force Imagery in Durkheim: The Integration of Theory, Metatheory, and Method." *Sociological Theory, vol. 3*, number 1 (Spring): 74–88.

Thompson, Kenneth. 1998. "Durkheim and Sacred Identity." In *On Durkheim's Elementary Forms of Religious Life*, eds. N. J. Allen, W.S.F. Pickering, and W. Watts Miller, pp. 92–104. London: Routledge.

Tilly, Charles. 1981. *As Sociology Meets History*. New York: Academic.

Timasheff, Nicholas S. 1957. *Sociological Theory: Its Nature and Growth*. Revised edition. New York: Random House.

Turner, Jonathan H., Leonard Beeghley, and Charles H. Powers. 2002. *The Emergence of Sociological Theory, 5th ed*. Belmont, CA: Wadsworth Thomson Learning.

Veblen, Thorstein. 1979. *The Theory of the Leisure Class*. New York: Penguin.

Wallace, Walter L. 1983. *Principles of Scientific Sociology*. New York: Aldine.

————. 1994. *A Weberian Theory of Human Society: Structure and Evolution*. New Brunswick, NJ: Rutgers University Press.

Weber, Max. 1946. *From Max Weber: Essays in Sociology*, eds. H. H.Gerth and C. Wright Mills. New York: Oxford University Press.

———— 1958. *The Protestant Ethic and the Spirit of Capitalism*. New York: Scribners.

———— 1978. *Economy and Society*, 2 vols. Berkeley: University of California Press.

Wiley, Norbert. 1987. "Introduction." In *The Marx-Weber Debate*, ed. Norbert Wiley, pp. 7–27. Newbury Park, CA: Sage.

Znaniecki, Florian. 1952. *Cultural Sciences: Their Origin and Development.* Urbana, IL: University of Illinois Press.

Websites

Alex Catalogue of Electronic Texts
http://infomotions.com/alex/?cmd=names&ltr=A

August Comte and Positivism
http://membres.multimania.fr/clotilde/

Blackwell Encyclopedia of Sociology Online
http://www.sociologyencyclopedia.com/public/

Dead Sociologists Society
http://media.pfeiffer.edu/lridener/DSS/DEADSOC.HTML

Émile Durkheim Archive
http://durkheim.itgo.com/main.html

George's Pages, the Mead Project Website
http://www.brocku.ca/MeadProject/

History of Sociology Section of the American Sociological Association
http://www.mtholyoke.edu/courses/etownsle/HOS/

Internet Archieve
https://archive.org/details/historyoftradeu00pass

Les Classiques des science sociale
http://classiques.uqac.ca/index.html

Open Library
https://openlibrary.org/

Project Gutenberg
http://www.gutenberg.org/

Marx & Engels Internet Archive
http://www.marxists.org/archive/marx/

Sociosite: Famous Sociologists
http://www.sociosite.net/topics/sociologists.php

Theory Section of the American Sociological Association
http://www.asatheory.org/

Thorstein Veblen
http://socserv.socsci.mcmaster.ca/~econ/ugcm/3ll3/veblen/

Verstehen: The Sociology of Max Weber
http://www.faculty.rsu.edu/~felwell/Theorists/Weber/Whome.htm

WWW Virtual Library: Sociology: Sociological Theory and Theorists
http://socserv.mcmaster.ca/w3virtsoclib/theories.htm

www.ingramcontent.com/pod-product-compliance
Lightning Source LLC
Chambersburg PA
CBHW021908020426
42334CB00013B/512